Praise

'Faye Allen has been indefatigable in her efforts to raise awareness around, and support for, women working in construction, in all roles and at all levels. Read this book and get on board with helping to create the construction industry of the future – more diverse, more sustainable and consistently building a product of which every industry participant can be proud.'
— **David Savage**, Partner, Head of Construction, Engineering and Projects, Charles Russell Speechlys LLP

'Faye's research shows how far we still have to go for true equality. This book is a powerful reminder of the strength, resilience and determination of women in construction. It shows the challenges they face and celebrates their unwavering commitment to breaking down barriers and building a more equal and inclusive future. It's a must-read for anyone who wants to make our industry fit for the future.'
— **Steffan Battle**, Managing Director, Wates Construction

'This book tackles a crucial issue with clarity and impact, presenting the challenges women face in construction, and providing solutions, in ways that are both compelling and accessible. It equips readers with the knowledge and insight needed to drive

meaningful change, empowering everyone to take action and improve the industry for the better.'
 — **Amy Bonczyk**, Chartered Quantity Surveyor and Adjudicator, MCMS Limited

'*Building Women* is a long overdue book that not only highlights the historic and persistent challenges for women in the construction industry, but delivers recommendations on how to tackle them in ways that enable everyone to thrive. Faye Allen makes a deliberate point of bringing those that don't identify as women into the conversation, because meaningful change for everyone requires everyone to get involved and lead in ways both big and small. This book isn't just about women or for women, it should be read and actioned by everyone.'
 — **Sybil Taunton**, Diversity, Equity and Inclusion Leader, Royal Institution of Chartered Surveyors

'What flows through this whole fascinating book is how much Faye cares about the industry she has worked in for three decades. Combining groundbreaking research, input from other prominent voices and her own unique insights, the result is more than just a book; it's a manifesto for a better vision for everyone who works in the built environment.'
 — **Jeremy Stockdale**, CEO, Ylead

FAYE ALLEN

Building Women

How *everyone* in construction can win

Re think

First published in Great Britain in 2025
by Rethink Press (www.rethinkpress.com)

© Copyright Faye Allen

All rights reserved. No part of this publication may be reproduced, stored in or introduced into a retrieval system, or transmitted, in any form, or by any means (electronic, mechanical, photocopying, recording or otherwise) without the prior written permission of the publisher.

The right of Faye Allen to be identified as the author of this work has been asserted by her in accordance with the Copyright, Designs and Patents Act 1988.

This book is sold subject to the condition that it shall not, by way of trade or otherwise, be lent, resold, hired out, or otherwise circulated without the publisher's prior consent in any form of binding or cover other than that in which it is published and without a similar condition including this condition being imposed on the subsequent purchaser.

Cover image © Shutterstock | elenabsl and robuart

Illustrations by Asis Patel

'Hard hat' icon by Sentya Irma, from thenounproject.com

This book is dedicated to all the friends, family and colleagues who have helped me throughout my career.

Contents

Foreword	1
Introduction	5
PART ONE Construction – What is the Issue?	11
1 The Construction Industry Is Great, So What Is The Problem?	13
Why is construction a great industry to work in?	16
Lack of diversity and aging workforce in construction	21
STEM careers aren't always appealing to girls and women	22
Retention of women in the industry	25
What do women want?	34
Summary	40

2 World Figures And World Issues – Gender Equality — 43

Global measurement on the lack of gender parity – bias — 45

Global issues of sexual harassment — 48

Does diversity increase profit and make better teams? — 52

Gender equality — 57

Gender pay gap — 59

Summary — 63

3 Why Do We Need To Solve The Issue In Construction? — 65

Construction skills shortages — 66

Women are capable — 69

Gender bias by design — 72

Pressure and mental health in construction — 75

Success like other industries/countries — 78

Work–life balance: The lost opportunity — 80

Summary — 82

PART TWO Women's Lived Experience — 85

4 Why Do Women Struggle To Succeed? — 87

Language barriers and double standards — 88

Women – confidence, bias and the battle to succeed — 92

Imposter syndrome and fear of failure	96
Programmes to 'fix' women not the system	101
The 'motherhood penalty'	103
Women's groups?	105
Summary	106

5 What's Actually Happening For Women In Construction? — **109**

Sexism and harassment	112
Bullying	124
Women who are hard on other women	135
Pay and promotion struggles	140
Motherhood and minorities in construction – the additional gap	144
PPE for women	148
Summary	152

6 Role Models And Practical Advice For Women — **155**

Women who do make it in business	157
Role models and allies in construction	159
Role models and advice from outside of the industry	167
Advice from the women surveyed for the book	173
What do women want from industry?	179
Summary	181

PART THREE Male Role Models, Allies, Institutional Change And Mentors To Women 183

7 How Can Men Help? 185

The patriarchy – what is it? 186

Male privilege – do men really have it? 192

Male allies – why be one? 201

Types of allies 208

What are the barriers to being an ally? 211

Summary 214

8 Institutions And Companies, Role Models And Allies – What Can They Do? 215

What are groups and institutions doing to make things better? 216

What are companies doing and can all of construction emulate? 223

Work with men to help them be allies 229

Male role models and allies in construction 231

Male role models and advice from outside of the industry 246

What can male allies do specifically? 260

Summary 264

9	**What Can We Do To Make Things Better?**	**267**
	Create inclusive cultures and behaviours starting with leadership	269
	Stop trying to fix women – offer development and mentoring programmes to men and women together	273
	Change the language	275
	Listen, educate and sell STEM	277
	Offer flexible working to allow work–life balance for everyone	279
	New ways of working in construction	281
	What can you do?	286
	Summary	295
Conclusion		**297**
Notes		**301**
Further Reading		**333**
Acknowledgements		**337**
The Author		**341**

Foreword

Has gender equality gone too far? Are men being discriminated against now? Is feminism destroying the very roots of our society? These are questions I am asked on a daily basis. As the founder and CEO of Male Allies UK, my role is to tackle misconceptions in a curiosity-igniting and non-judgemental way. From listening to women's experiences in the workplace to understanding how men engage with inclusion, it's clear there is a gap to close and many blind spots on which we need to shine a light. In our recent study, we found that 41% of men felt that gender inclusion had either gone too far or would be solved without their input. This statistic in itself showcases why this book is essential and why it has never been more important to get it into the hands of readers.

To be asked to write a foreword for this book was an emotional moment. While I have received the Freedom of the City of London for services to equality in business and been recognised as a gender equality changemaker by UN Women and *Marie Claire*, to be able to open a book for someone who I deeply respect and have collaborated with is an honour. Although my expertise runs across all sectors and industries, the conversations I've had in the built environment industry have been some of the most challenging but also the most rewarding. It is clear that access to valuable talent is lost due to misconceptions of how great it can be to work within the sector, and pockets of the industry are losing highly skilled women specifically due to attitudes and cultures that damage everyone.

Building Women provides insight, guidance and actions to ignite inclusion in the industry in a way that benefits everyone. You will find yourself nodding in agreement, scratching your head in disbelief and feeling inspired to initiate change. Whether you are a manager or leader, a colleague or partner, or a male or female, this book will open your eyes to things you hadn't considered and equip you with the information you need to take action. It provides not only the why, the what and the how that drive individual change, but also shows how to bring people together to be part of a collective movement. Whether you are interested in building skills, career progression, retaining talent or fostering innovation, this book will be a catalyst for the impact you desire, and provides benefits you didn't know you were looking for.

It is no surprise to me that Faye is the person who would bring this book to the world. Her knowledge of the industry is comprehensive and she is renowned for her commitment to building up other women, but most impressive is her continual desire to bring everyone on the journey, including those who haven't traditionally seen a role for themselves in becoming more inclusive. She has held space for courageous conversations, given grace while others have made mistakes and continued to take a balanced approach in the face of her own challenges. These topics can be something of a tightrope to navigate, especially in a divided society, but Faye does this with a poise rarely seen and in a way that holds dignity at its core.

Both the industry and the wider world are experiencing uncertain and volatile times, and it can be easy to shy away from these conversations and become inward-looking. This book will expand your perspective and equip you for the road ahead, no matter how rocky that may be.

Now is the time to be actively building the future we wish to see, and *Building Women* is at the heart of this project. Because when we build women, our systems become fairer and more inclusive. And when this happens, everyone benefits: women, men, the industry and wider society.

Here's to building women, and to continually building ourselves. Let Faye's words guide you, challenge you and inspire you. Let's come together and spread the message – once you've read this book, you will see what is possible.

Lee Chambers
Business Psychologist and CEO, Male Allies UK
Author of *Momentum: 13 ways to unlock your potential*
https://leechambers.org

Introduction

If you are a woman who has struggled to find your way in the built environment industry, you already know that being a woman in construction is hardly an easy career path to have chosen. Too often, despite working hard to succeed in construction, various obstacles may continually seem to appear in front of you to hinder your career progress.

Maybe it's the age-old challenge of being a woman working in a predominantly male environment and dealing with others' bad behaviour. Perhaps it's the glass ceiling, meaning that promotion and/or salary increases seem to continually elude you but not your male counterparts, or the fact you have had to move job numerous times in your career to achieve one or both of these things. Maybe it's the additional struggle for flexibility you have had when you returned to the industry post starting a family or while caring for relatives.

These struggles can leave women feeling marginalised, burnt out, anxious and lost, wondering how on earth they can move forward and succeed in their career.

Building Women will not only explain the issues women face in the industry, but it will provide guidance collated from the experiences of women in the sector to enable others to navigate these challenges and create the career they want. I have spoken to over 1,000 women for their perspective on how it feels to be in this industry. However, the simple fact is that this isn't only about women. Women don't need 'fixing' just because they work in a predominantly male environment. The environment itself needs to become more inclusive and supportive.

Part One of this book provides an overview of the issues the sector is experiencing. If you are a leader in construction, male or female, you will be aware and concerned that the industry is facing a huge skills shortage, with much of the workforce, particularly on site, aging and anticipated to be leaving in the next five to ten years.

The gap needs to be filled, and while the construction industry is becoming more diverse, currently women still make up only 15.2% of the workforce,[1] and most of those are in the more professional roles rather than trades, of which women only make up 2%.[2]

While women could help plug the gap, the construction industry also has a well-documented 'leaky pipeline' when it comes to retention of women. Even if we get more women into the industry, many leave.

Why is this? The answer, unfortunately, is due to issues such as discrimination, sexism, bullying, unconscious bias, lack of flexibility, performance bias and of course the dreaded gender pay gap.

This concerns me because I am passionate about construction. I have worked in the industry for thirty years. I started as a trainee quantity surveyor and have worked for numerous main contractors, subcontractors and consultants in my career and have spent the past nine years working as an expert witness in construction claims and disputes.

One of the things I love so much about the construction industry is that it's so diverse. No two jobs are ever the same. One year you may be building a hospital and the next you may be involved in a huge infrastructure project or building a school or a ship (or like me, now, dealing with disputes on these projects).

I love encouraging the next generations into construction with my STEM (science, technology, engineering and maths) work in schools, colleges and universities, but I also know that being a woman in construction is not easy and that the lack of diversity is a far wider problem than in many other industries.

The construction industry has come a long way since I started my career, when I was often the only woman on site and rarely saw another female aside from in administrative roles. However, the number of women in construction remains woefully low, and it saddens me that the industry is still haunted by lack of gender diversity.

In 2021, when I spoke at London Build on the diversity and inclusion (D&I) stage, it became clear to me that some of the same issues I've had in my career were still the same issues young women entering the industry now face. As if that weren't bad enough, it was clear from the conversations I had that day that women of colour suffered additional discrimination on top of that incurred by white women.

I realised that while I wanted to help women in the industry, it wasn't enough just to detail the difficulties women still endure. After all, that would not solve the huge problem of retention of women in the industry.

What was needed was for these experiences to be measured and detailed to help others working in construction to understand the challenges women face that prevent them from staying, along with some tangible solutions that could help bring about change and plug the leaky pipeline. Part Two of this book explores the experiences of women working in the industry and looks at what they think needs to be done to address the imbalance.

If the industry doesn't change, the consequences will be dire. In 2023, construction contributed almost £109 billion gross value added (GVA) to the UK economy.[3] Over the past few years we have seen the collapse of major contractors, an increasing skills shortage and an increase in the prevalence of mental illness. This, coupled with an aging workforce, is unsustainable and needs to be addressed.

INTRODUCTION

So how can everyone in construction win?

This is where the third part of *Building Women* – which looks at the roles of men in all this – comes in. To create a more diverse workforce we need male allies, role models and sponsors not only to support and encourage women into the industry but to help keep them there.

We need companies who are willing to think differently about recruitment and who are willing to introduce new ways of working to increase diversity in the industry.

Research (discussed in more detail in Chapter 2) shows that more diverse teams create more profit, collaborate better, communicate better, achieve more, are less litigious and are happier. Therefore the business case for diversity is sound.

Building Women will take you through a journey to lasting change by highlighting the issues in the construction industry, specifically looking at women's lived experiences and sharing their stories. We will look at patriarchy, the challenges women and men are facing and why women need men as allies to improve the industry.

Male allies can help change happen in construction by mentoring, championing and supporting women. They can challenge outdated behaviours, biases and attitudes towards women and, in doing so, can help to plug the industry's 'leaky pipeline'.

Being a male ally can be a daunting prospect as men may be concerned about saying or doing the wrong thing. Thankfully, there are many men who are already incredible allies to women, who are continually learning about the issues and who encourage other men to speak out and be supportive of women. Many of these men have taken part in my research for this book and I hope that listening to their experiences and hearing their 'why' will provide ideas and reassurance, encouraging more men in the industry to become allies to women to help create change to ensure everyone in construction wins.

We need to encourage more men to become allies to women to help promote gender equity and this book does this by providing a greater understanding of the rewards male allyship brings to both women and men. Making things better for women will not make things worse for men; if we improve the culture, things will be better for everyone.

If we all work for change together, everyone in construction can win.

PART ONE
CONSTRUCTION – WHAT IS THE ISSUE?

ONE

The Construction Industry Is Great, So What Is The Problem?

Construction is a varied industry and a key part of the UK economy, providing employment for over two million people. The industry affects everyone. It creates the infrastructure we rely on for the water we drink, the power we use and the modes of travel we take, whether that be the roads we drive on, the runways we take off from or the railway tracks our trains run on. It produces the buildings we use, like schools, offices, hospitals and homes. It is present all around us and used every day without us even realising it.

I've been in the industry for over thirty years, and I love the variety construction offers. As a quantity surveyor I've worked with many people on different types of projects over the years and I have never been bored, as no project is the same.

So, you may ask, if it's so varied and great, what are the issues?

The simple fact is that while construction can be varied and fun, it's not an easy industry to work in, particularly if you are a woman. As I know from personal experience, women are often treated unfairly despite working as hard and being at least as well qualified as their male counterparts.

I have, at times in my career, been on the receiving end of sexism, harassment and bullying and I had started to wonder how many other women had encountered similar experiences in the construction industry. Then the #MeToo movement gained traction in 2017, following revelations that Harvey Weinstein had been sexually assaulting and harassing women. This led to victims around the world sharing experiences on social media using the hash tag #MeToo – and with these two little words a global movement was born.

This was when I shared that I too had been the victim of a serious sexual assault by a work colleague years ago. I had never spoken of it to anyone, but in posting #MeToo on my Facebook page, I finally opened up about what had happened and proceeded to break down telling my partner and subsequently sought professional help.

However, it wasn't until I spoke at London Build 2021 that I realised young women were still struggling with similar experiences to those I had encountered in my career, and this was even more pronounced for women of colour or those who had become mothers.

I decided I needed to make the industry aware of the issues, good and bad, so that the industry I love so much can grow and not just *attract* women but, more importantly, *retain* them.

In my research for *Building Women*, over 300 women took part in an incredibly detailed survey questionnaire. Of these, 86% stated they were white/Caucasian, again reinforcing the need not only for diversity by gender but also in race/ethnicity. I did not ask about religion, sexuality, neurodiversity, disability or any other characteristics that may further marginalise someone and I recognise that there may be additional issues in respect of those characteristics that may warrant further research in the future.

How would you describe yourself?

White/ Caucasian	Asian	Other	Black or African	Middle Eastern or North African
86%	5%	3%	5%	1%

When I refer to 'minorities' in this book it is specifically in respect of the numbers based on my research, which show not only that *women* are in the minority by gender but also that the industry has an additional issue in respect of *women* being in the minority by race/ethnicity group as well.

The experiences described in this book are all real and are either from the women who took part in my survey or from women I have spoken to and interviewed as part of my research in the last three years.

They are experiences women in the construction industry have faced and are facing and oftentimes these experiences have remained hidden and gone unreported because women know reporting these things often means they come out worse off, potentially losing their jobs and/or career.

However, things will not change until we as an industry listen to the facts. The industry needs to hear about and, more importantly, learn from women's lived experiences so that change can happen and everyone in construction can win.

Building Women is therefore the culmination of my experiences and those of over 1,000 other women in the industry, as well as the input of some amazing male allies from various industries.

However, while this book looks at the issues women face, I also recognise men in the industry face their own challenges too. We lose two men every working day to suicide in UK construction so making the environment better for everyone is a priority. We need the culture to improve for all of us – so let's get started: why is construction great and what are the issues?

Why is construction a great industry to work in?

I have worked on many different types of projects across various sectors in the construction industry throughout my career.

Projects I have been involved in range from the construction and refurbishment of offices, schools, houses, universities, hospitals, religious buildings, power plants (including those producing energy from refuse), shipbuilding and sports stadiums, to aviation projects at airports for new passenger facilities and baggage projects, rail and infrastructure projects (including the construction of wind turbines) and even fertiliser plant projects.

I have worked on projects where listed buildings have had their facades retained with new floors constructed internally or on confined sites in central London where space is restricted and/or planning conditions mean noisy works can only be undertaken during certain times.

I have worked on projects that are live (schools and hospitals), with the added challenge of the public being in place while building is ongoing, and projects with contaminated ground requiring remediation, as well as projects with asbestos where specialist licensed contractors are needed to enable construction works to be safe.

I have worked on projects with basements, sub-basements and underground tunnels where permanent dewatering and backup was necessary, due to high water tables and aquifers, and projects with clean rooms where specialist ventilation systems and decontamination areas were required.

I have seen some amazing specialist trades, such as traditional stonemasons or wood carvers (who were flown over from Malaysia), and even worked with a specialist Islamic calligraphy writer in Turkey who recreated verses from the Quran for the inside of a mosque dome.

To me, the theme is evident: construction is everywhere, and it offers a huge amount of variety. Even now, when I work less on site on live projects and more in the disputes and claims element of the industry, I still have no concern of ever being bored as construction offers that constant stream of varied and different projects, even when it's narrowed down to projects with problems.

Then there are the multitude of different careers available in the industry, and that's where construction gets even more interesting! There are so many different careers and routes to take that it really doesn't matter who you are – there is something for you. Whether you want to be office-based, site-based, warehouse-based or a mixture, or whether you want to be creative or analytical or to use your hands, there will always be a place for you as the industry is so diverse.

For those who may not appreciate the full breadth of careers available, here are some examples.

In what are sometimes referred to as 'white collar' roles, we have those who work in offices and generally do not perform manual labour. Design-based roles include architects, engineers (eg mechanical and electrical engineers, civil engineers, geotechnical engineers, fire engineers, quarry engineers), acoustic consultants and technicians (eg CAD technicians). Project-based roles include estimators, purchasing managers, building surveyors, quantity surveyors, land surveyors, contracts managers, commercial managers, project managers, construction managers, site agents, site supervisors, and health and safety managers.

Then there are the 'blue collar' roles, the jobs that tend to involve a greater degree of physical or manual labour. This includes bricklayers, plasterers, tilers, welders, floor layers, painters and decorators, carpenters, cladding fixers, ceiling fixers, labourers, plant operators and mechanics, crane drivers, groundworkers, electricians, plumbers, roofers, scaffolders and window fitters.

Some of the roles may require degrees and specific professional training and later formal entry into specific institutions (eg chartered engineers, architects and surveyors) and there are many ways to get these qualifications. People can go to university post A-levels full time and join graduate schemes or get sponsored by companies to undertake training, for example by working four days and attending university one day a week to gain qualifications.

When it comes to trades which require specific training, people can undertake apprenticeships where they will be trained on the job and undertake the necessary vocational qualifications.

Personally for me when I started, I really did not want to go to university full time. I wanted to earn money so I could move out and have a car and so – thanks to my dad taking me on some site visits, which piqued my interest in becoming a quantity surveyor – I joined Try Construction (now Galliford Try) under a quantity surveying training contract. Under this contract I worked four days a week and then attended college and later university for the other day and the fees were paid for by the company. Later, when I got chartered and did my Post Graduate Diploma in Law, Wates supported me through the process and covered those costs.

Construction has something for everyone, whatever your preference, and this, in my opinion, is one of the best things about the industry – variety.

However, I can't pretend it's all perfect and it would be wrong of me to do so. As we will see through the rest of the chapter, the industry does have its issues and problems.

Lack of diversity and aging workforce in construction

The level of women in the industry remains low. The latest Office for National Statistics (ONS) data tells us that just 15.2 of the construction industry in the UK is made up of women (at December 2024). This figure, however, is not the highest recorded yet (that was 15.84% in June 2023), and sadly it has not improved meaningfully for over twenty years, with the average since 1997 being just 12.69%.[4] There have also been increases previously, followed by a drop again later so while it's exciting to see an increase, it's not guaranteed to stay at this level or continue to increase.

The Chartered Institute of Building (CIOB) statistics confirmed that while women make up around 15% of the UK construction industry, only 2% work onsite.[5] Further data revealed employees from different ethnic backgrounds and disabled employees make up a further 6% each of the construction workforce, meaning the industry continues to be predominantly comprised of white, non-disabled men.

The ONS data, however, has limitations. It excludes a large proportion of construction works that are undertaken 'off site' for things like design, planning, surveying, plant and equipment hire, manufacture of construction products and off-site modular build items. It also doesn't take into account the fact that a large swathe of the construction industry in the UK is made up of small and medium-sized enterprises (SMEs). Nevertheless, it does give us a good starting point for checking where we are in terms of gender representation.

The lack of gender parity in the industry is not a new issue. In 1994, Sir Michael Latham's report on the industry noted the underrepresentation of women and recommended that equal opportunities should be vigorously pursued, with co-ordinated action plans being necessary to promote equal opportunities and widen the recruitment base.[6]

While the lack of diversity is bad, the industry has further issues in terms of the aging workforce. CIOB statistics confirm the industry is comprised 32.5% of people aged over fifty and that retirement is imminent for 15% of that number.[7]

STEM careers aren't always appealing to girls and women

Many careers in the industry are in STEM fields (think design and engineering as an example) and sadly women remain underrepresented, but why is this?

The United Nations (UN) has set out seventeen Sustainable Development Goals (SDGs), number 5 being to 'achieve gender equality and empower all women and girls'.[8] In a paper published in February 2023, they cite numerous factors that cause the limited participation of women in STEM, ranging from social issues, societal expectations and family life to unequal workplace environments and lower financial support for research compared to that provided to men.[9]

There is no denying there are also negative gender stereotypes around intellectual ability that start young. In her book *Delusions of Gender*,[10] neuroscientist Cordelia Fine discussed her view that the majority of gender differences are not biologically wired but in fact created by social constructs and the environment we are in, meaning society and our environment as a child prescribes the gendered behaviour we follow (not our genetics).

Research in 2017 showed that by the age of six girls are less likely than boys to describe their own gender as 'brilliant',[11] and in 2020 a Fawcett report concluded that by the age of six gender stereotypes result in girls avoiding subjects they view as requiring them to be 'really really smart'.[12]

If a young girl believes she is less intelligent than a boy (self-estimated intelligence[13]) it's logical she will be less likely to pursue STEM subjects that may be seen as difficult or traditionally more for boys, even though science has established there are no significant differences between the male and female brain in terms of intelligence and girls often outperform boys.[14]

We all need to be aware of how young these gender biases can start. A great example of gender bias in young children can be seen in an experiment at a primary school where children were asked to draw a fire fighter, a surgeon, and a fighter jet pilot and almost all pictures showed men in these roles.[15] However, it is not just gender stereotypes; there is also a lack of awareness and many misconceptions around STEM subjects and the careers that are available, particularly those in construction such as engineering, where women remain in the minority.[16]

I'm a STEM ambassador (and prior to that a Construction Industry Training Board (CITB) Construction Ambassador) and I have always believed it's important for women in particular to go into schools, colleges and universities to bring awareness of the types of careers on offer in construction.

Young women and girls are often unaware of the careers available in construction or what STEM subjects they may need to study and some of this is because careers teachers are not always aware themselves. Recently I went into a school and, after my talk, the careers teachers said they had no idea there were so many career options and different paths to qualification available in construction. If parents and teachers are unaware of the breadth of careers available in construction, young people will not be pointed towards the various STEM subjects or apprenticeships that may assist them with entry into these careers (even if they do get over the gender stereotypes and biases they may have).

If we want to improve the industry, it's up to all of us to work on changing the culture and perception of the industry as well as educating people about the various opportunities the industry can offer.

Retention of women in the industry

Getting women into the industry isn't the biggest problem – keeping them is!

When I started in construction as a trainee surveyor in the 1990s it was because my dad got me interested in construction, but I was the only female on most sites (aside from administration staff/receptionists, cleaners and/or canteen staff). We even had a typing pool comprised of only women in the head office when I started. On my university degree course there were six women yet today I appear to be the only one of us still working in the construction industry in the UK, so why is this?

The perception of the industry years ago was one of 'hairy arsed builders' and dirty building sites. This has thankfully changed over the years and research in 2022 undertaken by construction data platform NBS of 2,000 18–29-year-olds found 56% of them considered construction to be an attractive career prospect and 57% of the female participants considered construction to be a generally 'diverse' industry.[17]

However, while this shows a promising change in the perception of the industry among young men and women alike, getting women into construction and engineering isn't the only problem we have; the bigger issue lies in keeping them there.

As an example, 84% of the women who took part in my survey said that they were often the only female in meetings with 77% of them saying this had been

BUILDING WOMEN

the case in the last year. It's hard for women to feel included when they feel so alone.

Things may have changed a lot over the past thirty years but one thing that sadly hasn't is the fact that we still have women in the minority. The 'leaky pipeline' means the numbers never increase for long.

There are many reasons for women leaving the industry, some of which I will explore further in Part 2 of the book, but here are some of the more obvious issues that make retention of women difficult:

- Discrimination
- Sexual harassment

- Bullying/harassment
- Gender gap affecting promotion and salary
- Incompatibility/lack of flexibility for childcare or other care arrangements
- Lack of adequate facilities in respect of women's welfare leading to feelings of exclusion

Several institutions have investigated these issues over the years. For example, in 2014 the Smith Institute stated in its *Building the Future* report that retention was a bigger problem than recruitment and the culture needed changing to aid retention of women, concluding there was a need for better conditions, flexible working policies and proper career pathways for those women who wished to go into management.[18]

In 2017 the Institution of Mechanical Engineers issued a report with the stark statistics that 'within a few years of gaining an engineering degree, just under half of UK female engineering graduates will have left the profession'.[19]

In May 2019, the CIOB provided a submission to an All Party Parliamentary Group inquiry, 'The Recruitment and Retention of More Women into the Construction Sector'.[20] This research stated women accounted for only 7% of the total CIOB membership and, of this, a large proportion were in student grades (suggesting an appetite for careers in construction and supporting the view that getting women into the industry is not the only problem). Of the MCIOB (equivalent to a bachelor's degree) and FCIOB (the equivalent to a master's degree) it was noted the numbers remained 'low' and that a large proportion were based in Asia where, culturally, construction as a career is seen in higher regard.

In June 2019, the GMB Union revealed figures at their annual Congress stating it would be *200 years* before the construction workforce achieved gender equality.

In 2022, the Royal Institution of Chartered Surveyors (RICS) undertook a survey on the gender diversity of its membership and the results showed that, while overall female membership had been growing steadily since the 1980s and had reached 18% (or one in five members), when looking at senior levels of the profession women made up only 4% of Fellow membership in the RICS.[21]

When the RICS looked at the longevity of female membership versus male membership in 2022 their research identified a leaky pipeline in the female membership where women stay members of the RICS on average for only sixteen years compared to twenty-eight years for men. When the data was examined further it showed that the average age for women's membership lapsing was forty-seven whereas for men it was sixty-one.[22]

These stats based on RICS membership clearly identify that women are leaving the profession much earlier than their male counterparts. While many women are starting families later, this age does not suggest this is solely related to starting a family.

Research commissioned by RICS in 2006 identified the top three reasons women left as being:[23]

1. The hours and conditions were too inflexible with the need to look after children (41%)

2. To spend more time with children/family (39%)

3. Restricted career progression and lack of opportunity (20%)

It therefore appears not much has changed in the past seventeen years as this latest RICS report shows the top three areas requiring development remain around flexibility, career progression and opportunity:[24]

1. More senior women in leading roles

2. Equality in pay

3. Greater flexibility in working hours

In 2024, Engineering UK research also evidenced the 'leaky pipeline'. This research revealed a decline in the proportion of women working in engineering and technology roles, reducing from 16.5% in 2022 to 15.7% in 2023 (a fall of 38,000 women) and their data said this decline was concentrated among women aged between thirty-five and forty-four.[25] Interestingly they also compared this to all other occupations and found no observable drop between these ages in other industries (further evidencing that retention is a serious issue in the construction, engineering and technology sectors).

There are many schools of thought that say representation means everything – that phrase 'if you can see it, you can be it' comes to mind. But how much of a difference can this make? Would the leak stop just because there were other female role models in high-ranking jobs who have overcome the issues and sometimes-entrenched misogyny women face?

I think looking to role models is not the (only) answer and here's why. First, while I agree role models are important, we cannot say that women can't and don't achieve unless they see another role model who has been on that path. There are plenty of women who have done just that, including myself, despite there being few or no role models to look up to, particularly in our early careers.

Secondly, we can't rely on more female role models leading the way as they will still end up hitting that glass ceiling, leading to burn out and/or walking out.

While role models are important and definitely help, it's the toxic culture and environment that needs changing to prevent the leak. We can look to examples and research from beyond the industry for further insight into what is happening within construction.

Look at recent events with women in positions of power. Jacinda Arden, the former New Zealand prime minister, said she no longer had 'enough in the tank'.[26] Scotland's long-serving first minister Nicola Sturgeon resigned saying the job was 'relentlessly hard' day to day.[27] Both these women were gender firsts for their nations and both were respected and admired. Susan Wojcicki, YouTube's former CEO, stepped back to 'focus on her family, health and personal projects' (sadly dying in August 2024 following a battle with lung cancer).[28] It is evident from their comments in resignation that these women knew what their best was and felt they simply weren't achieving it anymore and therefore chose to step down.

A McKinsey report in 2022 highlighted that female leaders experience higher rates of burnout than men do (40% compared to 33%), although their 2023 and 2024 reports found that the ability to work remotely or in a hybrid manner increased productivity and reduced burnout for employees.[29]

Women were found to be more likely to experience microaggressions, making it more difficult to advance their careers. The 2024 report noted that most companies offer bias or allyship training, but this does not appear to be translating into increased awareness or action.

The 2022 the report showed more female leaders were leaving at the highest rates yet and McKinsey found for every woman at director level who got promoted to the next level, two other women directors were choosing to leave their company. Women want flexibility, respect and fair treatment – and walk away if they don't have it.

Is this what happens with the leaky pipeline in construction?

Do women end up exhausted from the constant fight to progress their careers and then get to a stage where they are unable to perform at the levels *they think they should* (perfectionism), or do they feel that as a result of the lack of flexibility they have no choice but to step away from the industry? If so, what behaviours and attitudes might be creating the environment that leads to this burnout and inflexibility?

I know I have had periods in my career where things have been so difficult that I have walked away. The one time I formally complained about how I was being treated I was forced into a compromise agreement. Sadly I am not alone. Some of the women I have spoken to made the following comments, which show a systemic issue within construction where women are treated badly and then forced out if they complain.

> 'I had constant verbal sexual harassment then unfair dismissal after reporting.'

> 'It was so bad I had a nervous breakdown because of it...'

> 'I was constantly told I should "go back to my old day job". I was then made redundant even though others were less experienced and also clients had complained about them, which destroyed my confidence, and I left the industry...'

> 'Micromanaging to the point of me not wanting to go to work'

> 'Bullied by a senior manager for no apparent reason. Would berate me in the open office in front of the

team, very patronising and condescending. Ended up moving to another part of the office or working at home to get away. Ended up being scored lower on my appraisal as I "didn't handle situation appropriately", despite reporting to manager and HR. Ended up leaving the company.'

'I have very inappropriate comments said in very public and client faced environments where I have openly tried to address directly with the individual. I was avoided. I made a formal HR complaint. It's been added to my HR record. Nothing was ever done about it because I didn't put in writing anything formal like a grievance.'

'A new director bullied female professionals. He attacked me for being selected for a newspaper article on female professionals. He instigated disciplinary action against me for a non-existent "offence". He made the situation untenable and I resigned, having first secured another job.'

'I have been advised that I have cultural issues and do not understand the industry despite being in from grass roots level – if I pointed out errors, I was told not to rock the boat and even let go at probationary period for highlighting corruption in contractors.'

We will look at the reasons for these in Part Two of the book.

What do women want?

Women want to be treated with respect. Beyond this basic expectation, the main requirement that is evidenced in all research is flexibility.

Female leaders are about 1.5 times as likely as male leaders to have moved job to gain more flexibility or to work for a company more committed to diversity, equity and inclusion (DEI).[30] In fact 49% of women leaders place flexibility in the top three considerations when deciding whether to join or stay with a company, compared to 34% of male leaders.[31]

This comes as no surprise to me as I have moved companies multiple times in my career and not just to pursue promotions and pay rises but also to reduce commuting time or gain better flexibility and work–life balance. The fact is this doesn't just affect female leaders either; many men now also want flexibility.

The results of my survey of women in the industry in various roles, from trades and professional employees on site to those in more office-based management roles or business owners, show the need for flexibility across the board.

Flexibility is a priority for women in the industry, particularly those who are parents or carers. Here are a few of the comments women made in response to the issues they see and suffer in construction and what they want and need.

THE CONSTRUCTION INDUSTRY IS GREAT

'Flexibility towards parents, regarding attending school activities and children being off school due to illness.'

'There is very little flexibility when you are at site level; ie if your children need you I have found in the past being a single mum that you are expected to deal with any issues you have but there have been men in the same situation and they have been treated with more support, ie he's bringing his children up on his own, what a difficult job he has…'

'Benevolence bias needs to stop. We need to stop seeing mothers as the primary carer.'

'Meetings need to be during core hours 10am–2pm. Outside of these hours makes it very difficult for parents and carers. It is really, really important these changes are made for parents, not just the primary care giver, whoever that is. We won't reach equality until women and men are treated as equal parents.'

'Better recognition of struggles such as infertility – I worked through several rounds of IVF and eventually adopted. Adoption was treated as if it was less important than giving birth.'

'Perception that once you have children your career comes second. Realisation that men have as much responsibility for children as woman do. Balancing so that men and woman can both contribute to caring

> for their children. Flexibility for both parents regardless of gender.'

> 'While our company provides reasonable flexibility, the undercurrent is that you cannot be a mother and be a leader. Equal-opportunity education for all employees as mandatory in order to adjust subconscious biases would be a start.'

Women want flexibility and fairness at work, but they also want fairness at home!

I think if we are honest we all know that, traditionally, women have more often than not fallen into the role of doing the lion's share of the domestic labour at home. While my survey did not specifically ask questions in respect of the balance of chores at home a number of comments were made by various women I spoke to that covered just this, such as:

> 'Husbands need to step up. I cannot be wife, housekeeper, mother and engineer all to the best I can. Something always suffers.'

> '[We need a] culture that expects fathers to take as much responsibility for childcare and home burdens.'

In her book *Equal Partners*, Kate Mangino, a gender expert, tackles inequality at home where both partners work full time, enabling men and women to understand the default gender roles they may have fallen into and how it can be detrimental to both parties.[32]

THE CONSTRUCTION INDUSTRY IS GREAT

For example, have you thought about cognitive labour and how much energy it takes? Consider some of these thoughts:

- *What's in the fridge for dinner?*
- *What do I need to go shopping for?*
- *What will we buy X for his birthday?*
- *Who's picking the kids up?*
- *When are we meeting XYZ for dinner, and what will we cook or are we going out?*
- *Who's arranging the holiday?*

Now ask yourself, who in your household is the one who will generally have these thoughts?

Men are often pigeonholed into the role of the provider, the one who must look after and provide for their family, be the strong one, do the physical chores (mowing the lawn, DIY, putting out the bins etc). Often this means women will do more, as the cooking and cleaning jobs will be daily chores as opposed to weekly, monthly or one-off chores.

In the UK, women's share of the housework and childcare grew during the Covid-19 pandemic, with many expected to look after and/or homeschool children while trying to hold down their full- or part-time jobs.[33] Women were found to be undertaking, on average, two-thirds more of the childcare duties per day than men. In households with children under five years of age, women averaged 78% more childcare than men.[34]

This added stress on top of the already unbalanced burden of responsibilities at home led to mass burnout and huge numbers of women leaving jobs the world over.

A poll in 2023 revealed that housework and childcare in the UK remains unequally split between women and men.[35] The British Social Attitudes Survey, which has been going for forty years, found that while more than three-quarters of those surveyed said domestic labour should be split, 63% of women reported they were still doing more than their fair share of cleaning and cooking at home.

We have to ask why women are seen as the default caregivers and respected for it yet conversely if a man chooses to do that role it can be the opposite and they may be seen as weak or lazy or get mocked for taking that decision.

This is inequality and, while the balance appears to be better in same-sex relationships, getting the balance right at home is just as important as fighting for the balance to be right at work and in society at large for men, women and all diverse groups.

Gender inequality also affects men, particularly when they do not conform to traditional gender roles. Look at a man who chooses to stay at home to look after the children as an example. He may be mocked, seen as weak or suffer name-calling or comments about 'sitting around at home all day'. Men are often discriminated against when they take on this role, yet a woman who stays at home to look after children is not seen as weak or lazy.

Why, in 2024, did a man have to take his employer to court for sex-based harassment after his colleagues 'gossiped' about him working flexible hours following the birth of his daughter?[36]

In 2024 we should not be in a situation where women are treated differently and unable to pursue careers they love because they chose to have children or where men are mocked because they want more flexibility to parent or indeed to stay at home and be the primary carer to their children.

Even if women have a good home balance and do not have issues with children or caring responsibilities, they often spend additional time and energy on DEI work (which is often not recognised) because they want to help create a different culture at work.

Things are changing with younger generations. Recent research by generations expert Dr Eliza Filby pinpointed an issue where we now have middle-class GenZ women in their teens and twenties wanting greater work–life balance as a result of seeing the way their pioneering feminist Gen X role-model mothers dedicated themselves to their professional careers, breaking barriers and smashing glass ceilings, often at the expense of their fertility or family obligations.[37] Upcoming generations want flexibility and a better culture.

The only way things will improve for everyone is for there to be true balance and equity for everyone.

Summary

In this chapter we looked at the diverse careers available in construction and the role the industry plays in the UK economy. We also improved our understanding of the issues the construction industry has faced – and continues to face. In particular, we have seen there is a lack of diversity, with only 15.2% of the UK construction industry being made up of women and an average that has never exceeded 13% in twenty years. Data has also shown a lack of ethnic/racial and disability diversity, meaning we have an issue with diversity as a whole.

The industry is suffering from skills shortages. Reasons include an aging workforce, a lack of diversity and a lack of flexibility for those in the industry. The low rate of women coming into the industry, in comparison to men, is partly a result of underrepresentation in STEM fields. This, in turn, is due to a combination of social issues, biases and negative gender stereotypes that start at a young age and often have a profound effect on children by the time they are six or seven years old.

Research shows that the industry is starting to be considered more diverse. For women who do make it into the industry, it's still not easy or as inclusive as it needs to be.

Women (and men) want flexibility and fairness, particularly the younger upcoming generations. Construction needs to work harder to provide a more flexible and inclusive industry for them.

These issues all compound the industry's leaky pipeline, where we haemorrhage women. While role models can help women to enter the industry, it's the culture that needs to change to ensure they stay.

TWO
World Figures And World Issues – Gender Equality

The issues around gender equality are not restricted to industries like construction, although it is recognised that industries related to many STEM subjects appear to be more affected when it comes to the lack of women. Gender equality raises many issues and is a global concern.

This chapter aims to give you, the reader, a flavour of gender equality (or inequality) globally. If you already know the issues or would rather stick to construction-specific information and statistics, feel free to move on to Chapter 3. For those who want to understand the global picture, we start with the Beijing Declaration and Platform for Action on Women (BDfA) resolution.[38] Adopted in 1995 by the UN and 189 member states, the resolution identified twelve key areas where progress was urgently needed to ensure greater equality and opportunities for women and men, girls and boys.

In 2006, recognising issues with equality, the World Economic Forum introduced 'The Global Gender Gap Index', providing a framework for capturing levels of gender-based disparity and tracking their progress. Its 2022 *Global Gender Gap Report* reported that the global gender gap had been closed by 68.1% – meaning that it would take another 132 years to reach full parity – and that, while overall gender parity had improved since the first edition in 2006, progress had stalled in most countries and some were in decline.[39]

The report found that while no country had achieved total parity the top ten economies had closed at least 80% of their gender gaps. Iceland achieved 90.8% and had the best gender parity, followed closely by other Scandinavian countries in the top ten such as Finland (86%, second), Norway (84.5%, third) and Sweden (82.2%, fifth) and other European countries such as Ireland (80.4%) and Germany (80.1%) in ninth and tenth positions.

In the 2023 report, the gap had closed to 68.4% for all 146 countries and when comparing the 102 countries continuously covered since 2006, the gap was 68.6%, which only recovered it to the levels reported in 2020.[40] Again no country had achieved full gender parity, but the top nine countries (Iceland, Norway, Finland, New Zealand, Sweden, Germany, Nicaragua, Namibia and Lithuania) had closed at least

80% of their gap and for the fourteenth consecutive year Iceland took pole position with 91.2% and as the only country to have closed more than 90% of its gender gap.

As I write this, the 2024 report has been published showing it will be another five generations before gender parity is reached.[41] It shows an increase in closing the gap, for all 146 countries, of 68.5% so a minimal improvement in the last year. The 2024 report estimates a total of 134 years to reach full parity so around five generations beyond the UN's 2030 SDG target. Iceland was again ranked first and had closed the gap further to 93.5%.

It's therefore evident we have global issues; it's not just specific to certain industries.

Global measurement on the lack of gender parity – bias

One of the things that affects us all is bias. We will all have some forms of bias; some will be conscious and others subconscious. Many are deep rooted and come from hundreds of years of social, political and economic 'norms' that may have changed as humanity has evolved.

There are many books written on the subject of bias, and it could easily take up a huge chunk of mine. I will therefore touch on the subject, which is a theme throughout the book, and suggest you take a look at this in more detail if it resonates with you.

There are a number of generally recognised types of bias but the ones I am concentrating on throughout the book are the unconscious biases that we all have. The most common include gender bias, racial bias, age bias, confirmation bias, Halo effect, Horn effect, similarity bias, authority bias, beauty bias and performance attribution bias.

These unconscious biases are beliefs we have about different groups of people yet are often unaware of. Our brain uses them to speed up the processing of information it receives, and they will be wired in based on our previous experiences, social constructs and culture we have lived in.

In 2020, the UN Development Programme published a report following analysis of data from seventy-five countries that are home to over 80% of the global population.[42] This report uses GSNI, a social norms index, to capture how social beliefs can obstruct gender equality along four dimensions (political, educational, economic and physical integrity), providing evidence on prevalence of biases and measuring how they are evolving.[43] The report revealed that almost 90% of all people have 'a deeply ingrained bias' against women. Almost half of the people polled felt men were superior political leaders and over 40% believed men make better business executives.

The updated 2023 report (capturing data up to 2022) found gender bias remains a problem worldwide. The index covers 85% of the world population and revealed that close to nine out of ten men *and* women still hold fundamental biases against women and that these biases were across all regions, incomes, levels of development and culture, showing this is a global issue.

Shape Talent research in 2022 looked at everyday gender biases and sexism and found 47% of women face everyday sexism and microaggressions, with 21% believing harassment is not dealt with properly.[44]

Gender bias affects us all. I remember an exercise Dr Anne Whitehouse did with a group I was in a few years ago where she asked us to close our eyes and, as she read out various different professions, to say the first thing that popped into our heads. She read out professions like doctor, fire fighter and solicitor and I was shocked that my own brain showed me a man first before my mind kicked in with, 'Yes, but women can do that too.'

In 2022, the UN also reported that at the current rate of progress, it may take another 286 years to achieve gender equality for women and girls, confirming women remain the minority in STEM education and that globally women make up only 19.9% of science and engineering professionals.[45] Therefore there is still bias when it comes to women and STEM subjects, as discussed in Chapter 1.

Based on the development of the global average scores for each sub-index over the past sixteen editions for the constant sample of 102 countries,[46] at the current rates of progress, it will take 155 years to close the Political Empowerment gender gap, 151 years for the Economic Participation and Opportunity gender gap, and 22 years for the Educational Attainment gender gap. The time to close the Health and Survival gender gap remains undefined as its progress to parity has stalled.

Gender bias is a world issue, not just an industry issue and it's not limited to men, women have it too. In fact, the UN analysis in 2023 showed that almost nine out of ten men and women held fundamental biases against women and there had been little change in over a decade.[47] In the UN's 2024 SDG report specifically on SDG 5 (Gender Parity) it states it will take another 176 years to achieve gender parity, arguing that 'strong and sustained commitments to changing biased social norms, eliminating harmful practices and abolishing discriminatory laws are urgently needed'.[48]

Global issues of sexual harassment

Sexual harassment is another issue that is a global problem. Again, while it can affect both men and women, statistically women suffer from it more. The World Health Organization (WHO) analysis of data in 2018 across 161 countries found that worldwide nearly one in three women (30%) have been subjected to physical and/or sexual violence by an intimate partner or non-partner, or both, at least once in their life.

The WHO statistics do not include sexual harassment, which is something women regularly have to deal with. A 2019 study on sexual harassment and assault in the USA found that nationwide 81% of women and 43% of men reported they had experienced some form of sexual harassment and/or assault in their lifetime.[49] The more detailed statistics found 49% of women and 21% of men had been sexually touched in an unwelcome way and 40% of women and 21% of men had experienced some form of cyber sexual harassment. Overall, almost 20% of women said they had experienced sexual harassment in the last six months.

I particularly liked the table of categorisations used in this study as it defines what can be sexual harassment. This is especially important when we look at industries like construction that often use the phrase 'it's just banter' as an excuse for unacceptable behaviour.

In 2020, one in four women (25%) and one in six men (17%) in Canada reported sexual harassment in their workplace during the previous year.[50] One in ten women experienced gender-based discrimination at work and this increased for LGBTQIA+ communities.[51] This survey also found inappropriate sexualised behaviour was more common for women in occupations historically held by men.

In 2022 the Australian Human Rights Commission undertook their fifth survey on sexual harassment in the workplace that revealed one in three workers in Australia reported having experienced sexual harassment in their workplace in the last twelve months.[52] This research showed women (41%) were more likely than men (26%) to experience harassment and that over three-quarters of harassers were men (77%). The statistics got worse for Aboriginal and Torres Strait Islander people, young people, LGBTQIA+ people or those with disabilities or from other diverse backgrounds.

In the United Kingdom the *2020 Sexual Harassment Survey* undertaken by the Government Equalities Office of over 12,000 individuals found 72% of the UK population had experienced at least one form of sexual harassment in their lifetime and that two in five (43%) had experienced at least one sexual harassment behaviour in the last twelve months.[53] The three most commonly experienced sexual harassment behaviours were unwelcome sexual jokes, staring or looks, and sexual comments.

The research found that certain demographic groups were more likely to have experienced at least one form of sexual harassment in the last twelve months and 75% of those who had experienced sexual harassment felt at least one protected characteristic was a factor in their harassment (protected characteristics include things such as age, sex, disability, race).

For workplace sexual harassment, both men and women experienced this, with 30% of women and 27% of men reporting (although it should be noted that different types of sexual harassment were experienced).

Sadly, sexual harassment is everywhere and it's not just confined to one industry either; there are reports of it globally in politics (think Donald Trump or various UK MPs),[54] in TV and film (think Harvey Weinstein, Bill Cosby or Jimmy Savile), in sport (think Mike Tyson, Phil Taylor or James Owen).[55] We even saw it publicly on the world stage when Luis Rubiales, the now ex-President of the Spanish Football Association, kissed the Spanish national player Jenni Hermoso on the lips at the Women's World Cup final in 2023 (and saw the 'gaslighting' and denials of any wrongdoing afterwards although he has now been found guilty[56]). Even in 2024, the BBC chose to employ a known abuser and Andrew Tate-supporter, Nick Kyrgios, as a commentator for Wimbledon 2024,[57] and Trump once again became US President in 2025. In 2023, the ONS looked at experiences of harassment in England and Wales and noted that more women than men (13% compared to 7%) experienced some form of harassment, with a quarter of those who had experienced sexual harassment saying they had experienced this at their place of work.[58]

Women are not the only people that deal with sexual harassment, and we must acknowledge that it is wrong regardless of gender. However, this book is about women's experiences in the construction industry. Therefore, while evidence shows it is a global issue, we will be looking specifically at the statistics and research on the prevalence of sexual harassment in the construction industry in more depth in Chapter 5.

Does diversity increase profit and make better teams?

There have been numerous studies and research on the topic of diversity by Deloitte, Boston Consulting Group, Forbes, the Harvard Business Review, and McKinsey and Company (and many more) on the correlation between companies having more diverse teams and having more innovation and increased profit.

In fact all studies show that the more diverse and inclusive a company is, the more innovative it is and therefore in some cases the more profitable it is.

A McKinsey report in 2012 looked at the executive board diversity (in terms of gender and foreign nationals) and returns on equity and margins on earnings (before interest and tax) of 180 public companies in the UK, France and Germany.[59] The results found companies who ranked in the top quartile for board diversity had 53% higher returns on equity and 14% higher margins.

In 2018, Deloitte presented eight truths about diversity following its work with fifty different organisations worldwide representing over one million employees:[60]

1. **Diversity of thinking is the new frontier:** The research showed that high-performing teams were both cognitively and demographically diverse and this enabled them to tap into additional knowledge and cognitive ways of thinking.

2. **Diversity without inclusion isn't enough:** The research showed both are needed to achieve better business outcomes and the organisations with inclusive cultures perform better.

3. **Inclusive leaders cast a long shadow:** Behaviours of leaders in organisations can significantly affect individuals' feelings of inclusion and this translates directly into huge increases in perceived team performance, decision making quality and collaboration.[61]

4. **Middle managers matter:** They are key to the success of organisations' D&I strategy and not all managers can be engaged in the same way.

5. **Rewire the system to rewire behaviours:** Diversity training is not the solution. While training can help, there are four proposed steps to system re-wiring which involve using data to identify leaks and bias and to then introduce positive behavioural 'nudges' and tracking the impacts.

6. **Tangible goals make ambitions real:** Targets can have an impact, but they can also have a negative effect with arguments over targets and quotas and allegations of reverse discrimination. Measurable objectives are needed, and leaders should be ensuring they are not just about diversity but also inclusion with recognition and reward, ensuring leaders are accountable for these goals.

7. **Match the inside and the outside:** Customer diversity is as important as workplace diversity.

8. **Perform a culture reset, not a tick the box programme:** It's all about the culture in the organisation and this often requires complete transformation. Many organisations do not comprehend the amount of change required and use only compliance approaches to D&I, which does not work.

They referenced companies like Quantas, who went from huge losses to record profits and becoming one of Australia's most trusted big businesses, with their CEO at the time citing their inclusive culture as being what got them through the tough times as the diversity helped generate better strategies, better risk management, more comprehensive debates and as a result better outcomes.

Boston Consulting Group (BCG) undertook a study in 2019 of over 1,700 companies worldwide which showed that diversity not only increased the capacity for innovation due to expanding the range of ideas and options available but also led to improved financial performance.[62] BCG reiterated the need to build an inclusive workplace as having diversity alone does not guarantee business success.

In fact the need to change the culture is paramount. *Harvard Business Review* published an article in 2020,[63] in which two scholars reflect on how well businesses have adopted and interpreted the principles they advocated in a 1996 article on how companies could reap rewards from increasing diversity by adopting an approach they called the 'learning-and-effectiveness paradigm'. This paradigm had eight preconditions to enable the paradigm shift and four of them involve culture.

Some twenty-four years on these same scholars stood by their original views and noted that the reason many companies were not seeing the benefits of diversity was because merely increasing the diversity of people by numbers is not enough to improve the firm's effectiveness or financial performance. Companies will not get any benefits from diversity unless they create a culture that insists on equality.

The International Labour Organization's 2019 report, *Women in Business and Management: The business case for change,* surveyed 13,000 enterprises in seventy countries and found almost three-quarters of those companies that tracked gender diversity in their management reported increased profit of between 5% and 20%, with the majority seeing increases of 10–15%.[64]

In 2021, BoardReady released its report, *Lessons from the Pandemic: Board diversity and performance.*[65] In this report the data showed a direct correlation between diversity on boards of directors and the performance of the companies they led during three recent years, including the 2020 pandemic year. In terms of gender, those with better gender equality on boards had better growth and performance. When it came to age, boards with younger directors also had improved revenue growth compared to those boards with median director ages of sixty-five or more. While race was more difficult, as the report noted most directors were white, it did find those companies with at least 30% of board seats held by non-white directors had a 4% growth in revenue.

So why should we want diversity?

Research shows companies with better board diversity and cultures are faster to react to adversity, have improved financial performance and find it easier to change when needed.[66] They perform better and are more successful.[67] Elf Beauty research in 2024 showed that diversity in the boardroom can have several benefits, including:

- 15% higher return on equity[68]
- 50% reduction in earnings risk[69]
- Improved better price to earnings ratios[70]
- Fewer lawsuits where boards have three or more women and/or minorities[71]

If we embrace diversity in all its forms and, more importantly, create the culture change that is needed to go with it, we will have better financial returns and happier people.[72] We will have people who can collaborate and express new and innovative ideas that would previously not have been heard and leaders who support continual learning and help create cultures where people feel included, valued, challenged and supported.

There is no downside to diversity, but diversity alone is not enough; the culture of the organisation and their policies and practices all need to be aligned to support, develop and promote diverse talent and inclusivity.[73]

Gender equality

We have looked at diversity but what about gender equality specifically? After all, that's part of the reason I started this book – I want to improve gender diversity in the industry I love.

Women make up almost half of the world's population, yet we do not stand on an equal footing. Women face barriers everywhere and the world loses out as a result. Back in 2015 McKinsey and Company reported that $12 trillion could be added to the global economy by advancing women's equality.[74]

The right to gender equality became part of international human rights law in 1948 when the UN adopted the Universal Declaration of Human Rights. This recognised that 'All human beings are born free and equal in dignity and rights' and that 'everyone is entitled to all the rights and freedoms set forth in this Declaration, without distinction of any kind, such as race, colour, sex, language, religion ... birth or other status'.[75]

On 1 January 2016, the seventeen SDGs of the 2030 Agenda for Sustainable Development came into force.[76] These goals, adopted by world leaders in September 2015 at a UN Summit, were a call to action for all countries to work to promote prosperity while also protecting the planet.

Goal 5 relates specifically to gender equality,[77] yet globally no country has fully attained gender equality; while Scandinavian countries lead the world in their progress toward closing the gender gap, even they have issues. In fact, despite having the best overall score for the fourteenth consecutive year, on 24 October 2023, Iceland's women and non-binary people undertook a full-day women's strike (the first since 1975) protesting about gender inequality. They were urged not to do any paid or unpaid work, including domestic tasks at home, to raise awareness that Iceland still has a gender wage gap and that 40% of women experience gender-based or sexual violence in their lifetime. Iceland's biggest gap is in the financial and insurance activities at 26.2% and it also varies between occupational groups, with the largest gap of around 21% being for technicians and associated professionals.[78]

The greatest gender gap is seen in the Middle East and North Africa. Their gender parity score is only 61.7% although the region has still seen an increase since 2006, advancing its gender gap score by 3.9 percentage points in that time.

When we look at women in leadership positions, the situation is grave: the higher up the seniority ladder, the lower the numbers of women. Globally, no industry has reached parity when it comes to women in leadership roles.

LinkedIn research shows that at entry level 46% of roles are held by women globally, yet as women climb the ladder to seniority the share of women in management roles drops to 35% and by the time we get to C-suite roles women hold just 25% of the positions.[79] When specifically looking at traditionally male industries like construction and manufacturing, LinkedIn research shows that the gap is even greater with not even two out of every ten leaders being women.

Women are underrepresented in leadership positions globally in all industries.

Gender pay gap

One of the things that comes up quite regularly in discussions about women and men and whether things are fair is the so-called 'gender pay gap'. So let's take a look at what this is and why it exists.

The World Economic Forum reports that since 1971 the number of countries adopting pay equity laws has increased from two to ninety-eight, although there are also regional differences in the uptake of these laws and it's worth noting that only one in five economies has actually legislated for equal pay for equal work.

Most European countries have some sort of pay equity legislation. The right to equal pay for women and men for equal work or work of equal value has been a founding principle of the European Union since the Treaty of Rome in 1957, and it has been unlawful to pay men and women differently for the same work for more than fifty years in the UK. Despite this there are still gaps today.

The gender pay gap is measured as the difference between the average hourly earnings (excluding overtime) of men and women as a proportion of men's average hourly earnings (excluding overtime).

The gaps are reported slightly differently depending on country/area but across the board there is a gap:

In the UK it is a measure across all jobs within an organisation and across all levels of the business, not of the difference in pay between men and women for doing the same job.[80] The gender pay gap is higher for 'all employees' than it is for full-time or part-time employees and this is because women tend to fill more part-time jobs, which when compared to full-time jobs tend to have lower hourly median pay; therefore, the clearest analysis is seen across age groups for full-time employees.

For example, while in the UK the gender pay gap has been declining, the ONS stats for 2023 still showed that gap at 7.7% (up from 7.6% in 2022).[81] The gender pay gap is largest among higher earners although this has decreased in recent years and it decreased across all major occupations between 2022 and 2023.

In 2023, for groups that are aged under forty years, the gender pay gap for full-time employees is lower, at 4.7% or below, and this has been fairly consistent since 2015. However, for those aged forty to forty-nine years, the gender pay gap for full-time employees increases to 10.3%, and the gap widens further for those aged sixty and over, increasing between 2022 and 2023 from 13.5% to 14.2%.

In 2022, women in the US typically earned 82 cents for every dollar men earned, although this rose in 2023 to 84 cents (or 16% less than men) on average.[82] However, the US reports the controlled and the uncontrolled gap. Under the controlled gender pay gap – which considers factors such as job title, experience, education, industry, job level and hours worked – a woman earns 99 cents for every dollar a man earns. The Center for American Progress projects that gender pay equity won't become a reality in the US until 2056.

In the EU, in 2021 women earned on average 12.7% less per hour than men and in 2023 the gap was 13%, meaning for every 1 euro earned by a man, a woman earns only 87 cents (although there are bigger differences when you drill into the various countries).[83]

The idea of equal work for equal pay is different to equal pay for work of equal value; for example, if you compare cleaners (generally female-heavy jobs) with drivers (generally male-heavy jobs) while the work is different you could consider the jobs to be equal in value. However, less than half the world's countries have mandated equal pay for work of equal value.[84]

There are a number of factors that affect the gender pay gap such as:

1. Women and men often work in different sectors. If we look at caring roles and teaching or healthcare as an example, a larger proportion of these roles are undertaken by women and they are often poorly paid in comparison to other jobs.

2. Parenthood penalty – mothers aged twenty-four to forty-four are less likely to be in the workforce compared to women of the same age who do not have children at home. If they are employed, they tend to work fewer hours each week, often working part time around childcare responsibilities thus reducing earnings. Fathers, on the other hand, are more likely to be working and to work more hours each week than men without children at home. The gap becomes far bigger for mothers who have taken maternity leave, and it affects their earning potential long term.

3. Unequal share of paid and unpaid work. Women generally undertake more of the unpaid labour (housework, shopping, childcare etc) and this may affect their career choices and time spent in paid employment. The impact of this was seen during the Covid-19 pandemic when the so-called 'double shift' was more prominent as women tried to work and undertake childcare when schools closed. In doing this as well as the usual unpaid work, many stepped back from work as they were burnt out.

4. Fewer women in the age forty to fifty bracket are seen in higher paid occupations (eg managers,

directors and senior officials), at an age where salary for these occupations traditionally increases.

5. In some countries women are restricted from doing some jobs. Often, dangerous jobs are associated with higher rates of pay, so removing these barriers could assist with improving the gap (although there is no guarantee that removing the barrier would mean women want to do these jobs).

It is clear that the gender pay gap is due not just to gender but a combination of factors. While some of these can be improved with specifically targeted actions being made by countries and companies (by improving hiring practices, flexibility and mobility initiatives), there are some issues, such as the low rates of pay in some professions, that are more difficult to resolve. We will look in more detail at how the gap is worse for mothers, for example, in Chapter 4.

Summary

We have looked at many issues women face worldwide, and these can often be more pronounced depending on where women live, their culture and the industry.

Globally, sexual harassment is an issue and in the UK 75% of those who have experienced it say it was a result of a protected characteristic such as age, sex or race. The most common forms of sexual harassment are unwelcome sexual jokes, staring/looks and sexual comments.

Women are underrepresented in leadership positions and still have issues around equal pay that have a knock-on effect for women trying to progress. By the time we reach C suite, the representation is a pitiful 25% at best.

We also see what a big issue the lack of diversity in all its forms is for business, as they miss out on hard cash with higher financial returns, lower numbers of disputes, and happier people. However, it needs more than diversity: there must be culture change and policies and procedures in place to support and develop diverse talent and targeted actions to improve the gap.

Over the last few years, gender equality has stagnated or declined, and no country is on track to achieve gender equality by 2030.

As I write this, the 2024 *Sustainable Development Goals Gender Index* findings state 'grave concern' that, if things continue as they are, gender equality will not be achieved until the twenty-second century.[85]

THREE
Why Do We Need To Solve The Issue In Construction?

We looked at the problems in construction in Chapter 1 and some of the potential barriers to women entering the industry as well as some of the issues they face that lead to the leaky pipeline.

We have an industry that is responsible for everything around us in one way or another, whether that's the roads or rail we travel on, the airport we fly from, the houses we live in, the offices we work in, the gym we go to or the leisure facilities we use and more. Yet it is also an industry that has been plagued with problems for as long as I can remember.

Some of these issues are:

⛑ Image

⛑ Low productivity

- Low margins
- Adversarial nature of the industry
- Skills shortages
- Lack of collaboration/learning from mistakes and improving for the future
- Issues with workforce – not just with diversity but size and skill set
- Fragmented workforce, where much of the industry is comprised of SMEs and sole traders
- Lack of flexibility
- Poor investment into better ways of working and innovation
- Poor mental health and high suicide rate for men (two men every working day die by suicide in UK construction).

While the list above is by no means exhaustive, there are specific issues that could and would be improved by bringing better gender diversity (and diversity full stop) into the industry.

Construction skills shortages

In 2024 in the UK we had a new Labour government who initiated a huge house-building programme to build 1.5 million homes over the next five years.

WHY DO WE NEED TO SOLVE THE ISSUE IN CONSTRUCTION?

This means the construction of 300,000 new homes per year, representing a massive 30% increase on the number of homes built in 2022–2023,[86] by an industry with huge challenges around skills shortages.

The construction industry has suffered from skills shortages for many years. Back in 1998 (over twenty-five years ago), the Egan Report found there was a crisis in training, with a 50% decline since the 1970s.[87] This led to grave concerns about skills shortages and recommendations that the industry needed to recognise people were its greatest asset by providing better site conditions, fair wages and better training and by treating them with care and respect.

Fast forward to today and, while some things may have changed, the issues around the skills shortage and too few people being attracted into the industry and trained to replace the aging skilled workforce still exist.

In the latest CITB Construction Skills Network five-year outlook, they identified the need for 251,500 additional workers by 2028 to keep up with construction demand.[88]

The skills shortage has been going on for years and is due to a combination of issues such as:

- Dwindling number of young people entering the industry
- Aging workforce
- Brexit – meaning the numbers of migrant workers the industry has traditionally been able to use has significantly reduced

- Lack of flexibility
- Gender stereotypes and biases
- Gender pay gap

So why aren't women being targeted to assist with the trades shortage in construction?

The percentage of women in skilled trades has shown very little change in the last decade and this is despite the fact that research by Trade-Up found that 25% of women surveyed said they would consider becoming a tradesperson.[89]

However, there are also barriers to people, both male and female, entering the sector, as follows:

- Access to apprenticeship schemes
- Access to work opportunities with existing trades people
- Expensive training
- Training taking too long
- Lack of flexibility

Trade-Up found the biggest obstacles for 53% of women when considering joining the industry was the perception that they would not have the right skills or meet traditional industry stereotypes.

There are people like Zoe Tanner, MD of SNG Publishing (home of the HIP Learner of the Year and SPARKS Learner of the Year competitions), trying to support the next generation of trades people. I spoke to her about the Female Skills live installation competitions, which she said were introduced due to the need to empower women and bring on the next generations of women in these trades.

The industry has a skills shortage so the importance of promoting trade career paths to address the skills gap must be a priority and everyone needs to feel welcome. The work Zoe and the colleges and industry do to open trades up to women is imperative.

There are some great advocates for women in trades working in the industry that I will go into more in Part Two of the book but we, as an industry, need to make construction a more welcoming and accepting place for women and all diverse groups if we are going to solve the huge skills shortages we have.

Women are capable

Women are more than capable of working in construction and that includes in trades on site (despite what some people may say). If we look at wartime Britain, when men went to war it was the women who took on male roles and there is no doubt that women did them efficiently. It is sad that, despite proving they could do these roles, these skilled women were expected to give up their jobs when the men returned home and often unskilled men were promoted into skilled positions over women, regardless of their actual ability.

Historically, construction was tough and physically demanding but there have been many advances over the years. We have modular building, modern methods of working and advancement in building services technology that mean many roles do not require huge muscles and hard physical labour anymore.

I listened to a podcast where Mica May, Head of Development at Stopcocks (a national franchise of women plumbers), was speaking about the empowering nature of trade work.[90] Mica is an advocate for getting women into trades and she points out that diversity in the workforce will help shift the industry into more eco-friendly practices.

I spoke to Mica about the issues women on the tools face and discussed the *Women on The Tools* 2022 whitepaper that Stopcocks helped produce.[91] This whitepaper found 78% of UK tradeswomen had seen or experienced discrimination and this ranged from negative comments and bullying to intimidation and sexual assault.

Mica's point was that we have a huge skills shortage and women can help fill that gap, but the industry needs to be more inclusive. It's also important to remember that when industry improves ways of doing things, it will improve it not just for women but for men too!

Technology is changing the way people work in the industry and it doesn't have to be 'brute force' anymore, but careers people often still say the industry isn't good enough due to their own lack of knowledge or unconscious bias.

WHY DO WE NEED TO SOLVE THE ISSUE IN CONSTRUCTION?

This lack of knowledge or bias is something I have found when I go into schools and colleges to do career talks. There is still a perception that construction is a dirty industry full of shouty men and that trades roles are only for low achievers or those who do not want to go to college or university. I always ensure I showcase the breadth of the career opportunities available and often have career teachers approach me afterwards asking for more information.

We need to do better at presenting the diverse opportunities available in the industry, but we also need to improve the culture and 'fit' for women and other minority/marginalised groups.

We still have 32.92% of tradeswomen saying they had no access to a women's toilet on site,[92] creating the need for campaigns like 'Release the Bogs' as launched by Katherine Evans' Bold as Brass LinkedIn group in 2024.[93] We have 78% of tradeswomen saying they have seen or experienced discrimination,[94] and 39% saying that they aren't taken seriously because of their gender.[95]

If we look at the professional roles available in the industry, again there is no reason women are unable to do these roles. Women are proven to be capable, but we still have a situation where the number of women choosing STEM subjects is lower than men, with only 35% of women choosing to study STEM subjects,[96] meaning parity in subjects like engineering and technology will take over seventy years to achieve.[97]

Gender bias by design

One of the things I probably found the most frustrating while researching the book was the number of things we construct and design with little thought for women. This is because traditionally things were generally designed by men with little thought to the differences between men and women (we will look at this in more depth in Chapter 5).

I'm sure post Covid we are all more aware of the issues around personal protective equipment (PPE) in healthcare, where female doctors were put at risk due to facemasks not fitting them properly, but why was this? Design of many things has traditionally been done by men, meaning women or those smaller than the average-sized man were at risk. This isn't specific to construction but affects other industries like the military and emergency services; for example, stab vests didn't accommodate breasts so didn't offer adequate protection,[98] and although new designs were brought out in 2023 there are still issues with breast pain and getting it out to all women police officers.[99]

How does this gender bias affect women when it comes to construction design?

Let's start with queues for ladies in public toilets at concert venues, sports arenas, offices, airports, even small local sports/village halls. We can see how this would happen when these facilities were designed by men who have little understanding of what actually goes on in a cubicle for women. Did you know that women take longer to go to the toilet than men do (partly due to women usually having to remove more clothes[100]), that we need to go more often due to our shorter urethras and that we may need to use sanitary facilities while we are in there? As a result there are often not enough cubicles for women as no account was taken for the additional time women may need when original designs were drawn up.

If we look at the design of public spaces, like underground pedestrian bypasses, bus stops and car parks, they are often poorly lit with blind corners, meaning women do not feel safe.

Parks often cater for men and boys – with sporting areas for football, BMX tracks or skate parks, which are often used almost exclusively by boys and young men – but little thought for anyone else, leaving others excluded.[101]

These issues often lead to women and girls avoiding certain areas due to feeling unsafe, taking longer routes or avoiding going out at night due to fears for their safety. I don't know of any woman I have spoken to in my life who doesn't find that the change in seasons, when nights get darker faster, adds an additional element of fear into her day. Having to walk to the car in a dark station car park or walk home in the dark can be terrifying, with many women clutching keys between their fingers and being on ultra-high alert; one in three women feels unsafe commuting in the dark and 85% would alter their commuting pattern to avoid the dark if they had that option.[102]

If we look at office spaces, also traditionally designed by men, they will often have temperatures for air conditioning set based on the metabolic rates of men, meaning women are often cold in offices and wearing jackets and cardigans even in the summer months.

Research has shown that a gender approach to urban planning, for example, can reduce crime. Susan Leadbetter, a transport planner at WSP, looks specifically at gender design and women's safety, having undertaken her dissertation research on women's safety on public transport. She co-authored *Solving Transport's Diversity Disparity: Gender*, a report which showed 94% of women felt threatened when using public transport and 81% felt unsafe due to poor lighting.[103]

The fact is we need to ensure design in the future is inclusive and safe for everyone. Having more women and diverse groups working in the industry means more diversity of thought in design and construction and this will be better and safer for everyone.

But how does diversity of people bring diverse thinking and new ideas and innovations that improve things for everyone, not just for women?

I was provided with an excellent example of how thinking inclusively can improve things for all after speaking to Jamie Fisher at Monument. Monument is a British manufacturer that has for five generations manufactured professional quality tools for plumbing, roofing and drainage. I spoke to Jamie about how a woman in a focus group had given feedback on the difficulty she had operating an 'olive puller' and the man next to her reiterated the same issue with the product. As a result Monument introduced an innovative power tool attachment for the 'Olive Puller' meaning it is now easier for *anyone* who needs to remove the olive.

We need diversity everywhere, and in construction we need it to help the industry to innovate and provide better ways of doing things. We have a huge skills shortage that needs to be addressed and as the example above demonstrates, innovative new ideas will create tools and systems that benefit everyone regardless of gender.

Pressure and mental health in construction

We are all aware a lot has happened over the last few years. We have had Brexit and the pandemic, both of which led not only to subsequent issues in getting materials but also to huge cost increases in some materials.

Then there have been economic issues as a result of tension in the Middle East and the war in Ukraine, which have led to higher fuel prices, particularly diesel, affecting the costs of heavy equipment like cranes and construction plant.

Add to this the huge shortage of skilled workers, harsh deadlines and often unrealistic budgets and it's easy to see the increasing pressure being put on contractors, specialist contractors, suppliers and sole traders.

As of August 2024, over 4,300 construction firms in England and Wales had gone into administration since 2020 and construction firms accounted for 17.4% of all insolvencies in England and Wales.[104]

In September 2024, the UK's sixth-largest contractor by turnover, ISG, went into administration, leaving thousands of people out of work, jobs halted, and specialist contractors, suppliers and sole traders unpaid.

Then we have had inflation and higher interest rates, causing a higher cost of living, and more recently a new government. All these things combined mean we have a 'people' industry that feels like a pressure cooker waiting to blow.

Is it any wonder, then, that we have a mental health crisis in construction? We have women struggling for various reasons as we will see in Part Two of the book. For men, particularly when you add to the above an often tough and demanding, sometimes physical, work environment, it's evident that things are not good.

We have an industry with poor payment practices, where people often have concerns about getting paid, trying to pay others and trying to make a profit, all while also dealing with some quite frankly dreadful behaviour towards them from other parts of the industry (think ridiculously long payment terms, contract clauses that remove rights and, often, people with a lack of knowledge tasked with running or administering said contracts). This can frequently lead to disputes and King's College London's report in 2022 found that 49% of disputes were a result of inadequate contract administration;[105] in 2023 this figure reduced only to 42% and the competence of contract participants was still raised as a top cause of disputes.[106]

This all happens while people are trying to work (including away from home), raise a family, care for relatives, deal with health issues such as chronic pain (a common issue in many trade roles in the industry), and keep control in other aspects of life. Therefore is it any wonder it's the perfect recipe for increasing pressure?

It is no coincidence that the expectations and pressures placed on men, who still make up the majority of the UK construction industry, can lead to mental health issues and illness.

The WHO has said suicide remains one of the leading causes of death worldwide.[107] While rates vary between countries, more than twice as many men die from suicide as women (although more women attempt suicide, so things are not good for women either).[108]

In the UK, the Samaritans found the highest suicide rates in males aged fifty to fifty-four in 2021, with males being 2.9 times more likely to die by suicide than women; if we go further and look specifically at construction (a traditionally male industry), it is hardly surprising that these statistics get even worse.[109]

In 2019, CIOB research found 26% of construction industry professionals had thought about taking their own life and 56% of them worked for companies with no policies on mental health in the workplace.[110] Some of this is because the UK construction industry is made up largely of SMEs and many self-employed people so many do not have the resources or indeed time and staff to put these policies in place.

Research by Lighthouse, the construction charity,[111] confirmed that suicides in UK construction are three times that of the national industry average, meaning workers in construction are nearly four times more likely to take their own life compared to workers in other sectors. In 2021 there were 507 suicides in construction; this is almost two men taking their own life every working day.

The statistics don't improve in the industry elsewhere either. The US reported their construction industry has one of the highest suicide rates among professions with an estimated 6,000 construction workers dying by suicide in 2022.[112] In Australia they lose a construction worker every second day to suicide with construction workers being six times more likely to die by suicide than from an accident at work.[113]

We need to make construction better for everyone to work in, not just to solve the skills shortage but to improve the culture. We must remember it's a people industry so that people do not suffer from preventable stress, become sick, suffer mentally or make that tragic decision to take their own life.

Success like other industries/countries

The construction industry is never going to improve and solve the skills shortage if it does not improve diversity and its workplace culture. For that to

WHY DO WE NEED TO SOLVE THE ISSUE IN CONSTRUCTION?

happen, it's clear that things need to change so what can we learn from other countries or industries?

One thing that could make a difference to the numbers of people in the construction industry, and to the retention of women in particular, would be promoting more progressive parental policies.

Norway offers multiple options for parental leave with one-year parental allowance and a further twelve months to be taken immediately after the first leave. Either parent can take the leave, including adoptive parents and foster parents, and there are various options in respect of 'parents money'.

In 2022, Finland introduced equal parental leave, changing it from 54 days' paid leave to 160, with both parents being entitled to 160 working days of leave each. A parent can give up a maximum of 63 parental leave days to the child's other parent and a single parent can use all 320 working days.[114] Since this change, fathers in Finland take almost double the amount of days off, now taking on average 78 days.[115]

This shows that if we offer men these options they will take them, and this could help with the issues women face where they, generally, are the ones who take the parental leave.

There are many progressive companies like Marks and Spencer who have gone further with their new flexible working offering 'Worklife', introduced to provide work–life balance. As part of this, they offer many work options, such as a four-day compressed week, a nine-day fortnight and the opportunity to job share, as well as introducing neonatal policies offering those whose babies require specialist care up to twelve weeks of paid leave. M&S also offer six weeks' fully paid paternity leave and they doubled their maternity and adoption leave to twenty-six weeks at full pay.[116]

Companies are recognising this need and as of December 2023 there were seventy-four UK employers offering equal parental leave.[117]

Introducing equal parental leave and allowing for different family demographics will not only help the families involved but will also help to change the stereotypical perception that caregiving or parenting is a female responsibility.[118] Studies have shown that when men take parental leave they are more likely to be more involved in the care of their children.[119]

Work–life balance: The lost opportunity

As you will see in Part Two of the book, flexibility is something that women have said they want and need, yet in construction it is often something that we are told is impossible to achieve, particularly in site roles as the traditional view is that we must have people there on the ground all the time.

I used to get to site at 7am–7.30am and leave anywhere between 5pm and 6.30pm depending on the job. My contracted hours were usually something like 8am–5pm or 8am–5.30pm and this would often include additional time for a long commute each way, sometimes driving in the car for over an hour or sometimes a combination of car and train depending on the site location. My worst commute was two hours fifteen minutes each way, bringing my working day to anywhere between twelve and fourteen hours; by the time I got home it was often a case of eat, sleep, repeat.

There was also (and still is according to women I have spoken to as part of my research) a stigma attached to not working longer hours than contracted. I remember well if I turned up at 8am (my contracted work start time) people on site would say things like 'nice of you to join us' or 'did you forget your alarm', or if I left before 5 (even having had no breaks all day) I would get, 'Oh, half day is it?'

This mentality and 'banter' are the reasons the industry is not attracting and retaining people in certain areas, particularly women who often have the lion's share of caring responsibilities and may need to get children to childminders or school etc.

For the industry to improve its retention of women and close the skills shortage gap it needs to take on board what women (and many younger and older generations) want – flexibility.

Flexibility has become a priority, particularly since Covid, and there are plenty of companies in other industries offering various flexible working options. Flexa researches and provides details of jobs and of the top 100 companies offering flexibility in the UK (and elsewhere) and scores them based on their flexible offering and transparency.[120] This includes top-100 companies like Mars UK, Centrica, Virgin Media, O2 and TUI Group, as well as construction consulting companies like Mott MacDonald.

When it comes to flexibility there is also tangible proof it can work. In a trial scheme run by 4 Day Week Global in 2022, sixty-one employers took part in a trial of a four-day week on full pay; yes, you read that correctly, 80% of the time worked for the full amount of pay. The results were big, and the biggest that may matter to employers – aside from the 71% decrease in employee burn out, 55% increase in work ability and 57% decrease in attrition rate – was a whopping *35% average increase in revenue*.[121] Best of all, 92% of the businesses involved planned to continue the four-day week and eighteen companies said this would be a permanent policy change.[122]

We already have some forward-thinking construction companies in the UK offering flexibility (yes, even for those who work on site) and I look at what companies in the industry are doing to improve flexibility in Chapter 8.

Summary

In this chapter we have looked at the issues the industry needs to resolve. We have also seen how the industry has been slow to embrace new innovations that could attract new talent and the gender bias in design that is prevalent in much of the world around us.

We have seen the impact from Brexit, the war in Ukraine, tensions in the Middle East, issues with inflation, and changes in government, all of which have added pressure to an already strained industry. Hundreds of companies have become insolvent. Add to this the everyday tensions in construction, with the deadlines and budgets squeezed to within an inch of their life, and we have an industry where mentally many people are suffering. Construction has one of the highest rates of suicide for men in any industry in the UK. The situation is dire and needs to change.

Other countries have recognised that to remove barriers for women, change in culture and policies are needed. Equal parental policies are a good place to start, enabling both parents to take time for children, sharing caregiving to help change traditional attitudes. Flexibility is key and construction could learn a lot from other industries and countries who offer this as standard.

PART TWO
WOMEN'S LIVED EXPERIENCE

FOUR
Why Do Women Struggle To Succeed?

Women face a number of issues that can lead to them struggling to succeed in their careers. Some issues are systemic and a result of the gender bias that is all around us whereas others are as a result of the experiences we have.

Women are judged more harshly than men and often treated like they are the 'problem' when issues in the workplace arise. We need to fix the systemic issues around us in order for women to thrive and be happy.

However, women also have particular issues that have occurred as a result of their own biases and beliefs and the conditioning around them that they also need to work to resolve.

These are issues women struggle with globally across all industries. In this chapter we will look at the issues both from society and from women themselves and consider what is being done and what can be done to improve the situation in the future.

Language barriers and double standards

When it comes to women struggling to succeed in their careers, one of the things that has come up continually in my research (and in my own career) is the double standards women have to contend with, particularly around language and behaviours.

Society still holds onto traditional gender stereotypes that associate women with qualities like empathy, kindness, gentleness and being nurturing, whereas men are expected to be assertive, masculine, confident and decisive. When women display assertive behaviours that challenge traditional norms they are seen as deviating from their expected role and are often labelled as angry or aggressive.

I remember being called 'rottweiler' and a 'ball buster' earlier in my career when working as a site quantity surveyor, whereas similar traits in men at my level meant they were called assertive, decisive and strong.

When I gave feedback in a professional but blunt manner I was called 'an ice queen' or asked if it was 'that time of the month', yet if a man was blunt he would be called an effective communicator who didn't beat around the bush.

Women are also underestimated and constantly judged as having less leadership potential than men.[123] Murray Edwards College's year-long research in 2018 found 74% of female employees said workplace culture made it more challenging for women to advance their careers than men and 42% of men concurred. It also showed women are judged differently for the same behaviour as men, with 43% of women saying they had directly experienced being judged more negatively than men for exhibiting the same behaviour in the last twelve months.

This is a theme that has continued over many studies. In 1995, research showed that women were considered less competent than men in stereotypically male jobs,[124] while in 2022 research found that people find it hard to imagine women as leaders because the qualities typically associated with leadership (assertiveness, ambition, competitiveness, confidence etc) are stereotypically associated with men.[125]

Mary Ann Sieghart refers to this as another part of the 'authority gap', where women are often judged and assumed to be less competent than they are and will lose out if they don't highlight their successes and achievements.[126]

When it comes to women's achievements this is something that Gill Whitty-Collins refers to as the umbrella theory,[127] where a disproportionate number of women think their work will speak for itself and fail to see that this is like doing work under an umbrella: management are unaware of what goes on beneath the umbrella – they only see the top. So while men often shout about their achievements and get seen by management as a result, women often don't. Women need to ensure they and their work is visible and need to be better at shouting about it.

However, having spoken to many women while writing this book, sometimes, even if women do shout about their achievements, they are still judged harshly. They may be seen as 'showing off' or being 'cocky' when publicising their achievements, meaning women sometimes cannot win either way. This is backed up by a 2020 study that found women in STEM who publicly spoke of their work in academic and non-academic settings were stereotyped as 'bitchy', 'bossy' and 'emotional' and often even by their own gender.[128]

Language is important and powerful, but the bias and judgements used can be detrimental. If we are to change and become more objective, we need to think about language use. Here are just a few examples of words used to describe behaviour with men vs women:

Man	Woman
Assertive	Pushy, aggressive, angry, shrill, argumentative
Ambitious, cocky	Selfish, power-seeker, vain
Direct	Curt, cold, ice queen, blunt
Deliberative	Indecisive
Arrogant, self-assured	Cocky, inept

Competitive	Ego-driven, opinionated
Inspiring	Excitable
Confident	Bitch, bossy, up herself
Passionate	Emotional, menopausal, time of the month, rude

We all need to think about our language and the biases and judgements we have about others, otherwise things will never change and these double standards will continue.

While a lot of the book has been about the issues women are facing globally and specifically in construction, it's time we also recognise things are not great for men either and that they too suffer from societal expectations and stereotypes. These issues and double standards also put pressure on men and no doubt in some part play a role in the horrifying statistic where two men every working day choose to take their own life in the UK construction industry.

There are ways in which men are less fortunate than women. Here are a few examples:

- Men are judged for expressing emotion due to societal expectations that they are supposed to be strong; these stereotypes affect mental health.
- Men often do more hazardous jobs, meaning they suffer from a higher rate of workplace injuries.
- There is an impression that men have limited support when it comes to men facing domestic

abuse or violence despite one third of domestic abuse victims being male.[129]

- Men are judged harshly by many should they want to be in more care-giving roles.

We will look in more depth at how these things and the patriarchy specifically affects all of us, including men, in Chapter 7.

Women – confidence, bias and the battle to succeed

We will all have different forms of bias but how does this affect women specifically? There is a great deal of research that suggests women are judged more harshly than men and that our social conditioning means women are not recognised for our credibility as easily as men are and that women often don't recognise their own abilities (whereas men often appear more confident and have no issues recognising theirs).[130] Add to these issues coming to work in a traditionally 'male' environment and it's hardly surprising women struggle… or is it?

Starting with women then, how do women judge themselves? What biases do many women in construction I have spoken to have against themselves? Almost every woman I have spoken to in the last few years at some point has mentioned confidence and many mention that, when it comes to changing job, they believe men apply for positions if they meet just 60% of the criteria whereas women only apply if they meet 100%.

Is this true, or have we been fed disinformation that makes us question our own capabilities thus affecting our confidence? This 'research' has been re-quoted in many articles, posts and even books but it has largely been debunked because there was no actual detailed research or substantiation behind it aside from a speculative comment made by a senior executive at Hewlett Packard.[131]

The Behavioural Insights Team research in 2022 found that women apply for jobs when they meet 56% of the requirements and men apply when they meet 52% and that in more qualified applicants there was no gender difference in willingness to apply.[132] Let's stop creating self-fulfilling prophecies and biases by repeating statistics that are not even based on credible research!

In addition to our own biases, we have the biases of others; in an industry predominantly made up of men, like construction, there can be a lot of bias to deal with. We only have to look at Mary Ann Seighart's research in *The Authority Gap* to see that women are still taken less seriously than men and that this can have a detrimental impact on their careers and confidence.[133] Not only do women deal with gender bias and possibly motherhood bias but some will face an additional racial bias, having their competency questioned even more often than white women do.

We see this bias in McKinsey & Company and LeanIn.Org's *Women in the Workplace* reports, which look at the 'broken rung' in the corporate ladder whereby fewer women than men achieve a first promotion to manager in a given year. Comparing results from 2018 to 2024, the first broken rung was again reported to be an issue for women overall; looking at the breakdown for women of colour, Asian women had made good progress, Latinas faced their worst broken rung in 2024 and black women's progress had regressed to 2020 levels.[134]

Women are constantly judged. They are judged if they are a parent (she can't do X because she's a mum and needs to deal with childcare), and judged if not a parent, being expected to do more or not take holidays at certain times because they must 'have more time'. They are judged on age, being considered too young and not experienced enough and then suddenly too old and 'menopausal' or an 'old bag' or 'aged', whereas older men are simply seen as mature and distinguished. If women are introverted they are not seen as potential leaders, but if they are extroverted they are viewed as aggressive. Women generally have to work harder to prove their worth and cannot seem to win. Is it any wonder women's confidence takes a hammering?

The fact is we see these judgements and biases everywhere. If we look at sport, girls often don't get into sports like football as they are often pushed into things like ballet, athletics and gymnastics, whereas boys are often pushed into team sports like football, cricket and rugby. While this is slowly changing, this has created years of bias making us unconsciously think if girls step out of what is considered the 'norm' and play football, for example, that they 'won't be or may not be as good as a boy/man will'.

This gender bias is seen in spectators; a Swiss study found men gave lower ratings when they knew they were watching women's football yet if players were blurred, so gender wasn't obvious, women's football was rated the same as men's.[135]

There are some people trying to smash the bias. For example, I spoke to Wayne Morgan, who started Gotherington Jaguars girls football team in 2019 when his daughter and her friend wanted to play but couldn't find a girls team.[136] One of their coaches posted on a Gloucestershire Facebook group, seeking venues to watch a Lionesses game, and was greeted with misogynistic abuse from men, prompting the coach to post a clip on Instagram about the popularity and success of the girls' teams within their club and women's football generally, which is worth watching.[137] For Wayne it wasn't just about his daughter wanting to play football; the team was started because he could see girls losing out on the opportunities that being part of a team gives them. He has seen the team building happen with the girls and watched their confidence grow and the team has gone from strength to strength. This is a perfect example of how we can challenge biases and create change if we work together.

Bias is a theme that runs throughout this book because it is something that affects all of us in various ways every single day. My ask is that each time you read about it you stop and think about the things you may do or say or even think in your daily life that are a result of your own unconscious bias and not a result of fact. Remember, once you have thought about it, if you continue to think in that way and not challenge your own thinking, the bias has actually become *conscious*, and that is not a sign of growth.

Imposter syndrome and fear of failure

Imposter Phenomenon, as it was originally termed by psychologists Dr Suzanne Imes and Dr Pauline Rose Clance in the 1970s, was based on a study of 150 highly successful white women who either had PhDs in various specialisms and were respected professionals in their relevant fields or alternatively were students who had been recognised for their academic excellence.[138]

The idea of this phenomenon was that these women were unable to accept their success, doubted their abilities despite their achievements and felt like frauds, fearing they would be found out. It also identified some associated clinical symptoms: general anxiety, lack of self-confidence, depression, and self-imposed standards of achievement they were unable to hit, which led to frustration (ie perfectionism). The original study was based on a small selection of white women and noted that while the phenomenon had been found to affect men as well it seemed less prevalent and required further research.

WHY DO WOMEN STRUGGLE TO SUCCEED?

[Illustration: a woman's face surrounded by handwritten phrases: "THEY ARE NEVER GOING TO PICK YOU", "YOU ARE NOT WORTH IT", "YOU ARE NEVER GOING TO GET A RISE", "THEY ARE ALL GOING TO KNOW YOU ARE NOT GOOD ENOUGH". Signed Avis Patel.]

Fast forward to 2024 and there have been hundreds of studies into the issue and many famous women have admitted feeling it (Sheryl Sandberg, Michelle Obama, Ellie Goulding to name just a few); this is despite the fact that most groups were excluded from the study, such as women of colour, people of different genders, people with different professional backgrounds and social economic upbringings.

We know there are issues in the world due to events throughout history that have impacted people and created bias and various 'isms'. Issues like sexism, classism, racism, xenophobia and transphobia, for example, all have a part to play, yet none of these issues were specifically identified or even considered as part of the original study, so how can we say it only or mainly affects women and does not affect men as well?

Mary Ann Sieghart refers to imposter syndrome as having the underlying issue of a lack of self-confidence and as her research showed the continuous 'mandermining of women's ability is bound to dent their intellectual confidence'.[139]

The fact is most people I speak to regardless of gender, race or social background admit that they have feelings of not being good enough or wondering how on earth they got to where they are and *all* the people I spoke to said it made them feel anxious at times and question their own abilities (although I do note that the men I spoke to did not seem to have as high an amount of anxiety as the women did but they still felt it).

I, too, have felt these feelings but I started questioning whether it was really something that meant I needed 'fixing' – as is suggested by study after study which directs you to go on a leadership course, go on a confidence course, get a mentor, pretend you don't have it, act like a man, be assertive, stand up for yourself, etc – or whether the environment I was in needed fixing, particularly in a predominantly male industry like construction?

More recent research has suggested this is in fact the case; Harvard recently issued a paper where they called out the issue, aptly named 'Stop telling women they have imposter syndrome'.[140]

Feelings of uncertainty are an expected and normal part of professional life so why are women who experience these feelings labelled and why are workplaces continuing to allow systems of discrimination and abuses of power which affect all individuals but particularly those from minority groups to continue?

Reshma Saujani recently gave a talk to the class of 2023,[141] where she likened 'imposter syndrome' to something called 'bicycle face' that afflicted only women in the 1890s should they ride a bicycle.[142] Reshma referred to this as being a form of control at the time to prevent women from having the new-found freedom the bicycle gave them and it was a result of men wanting to scare them from riding.

Bicycle face was debunked in 1897 by doctor Sarah Hackett Stevenson when she stated that the painful anxious face was only seen in beginners and amateurs and once the rider became proficient the look passed away.[143]

So should we debunk 'imposter syndrome' and treat it like bicycle face, as Reshma Saujani suggested in her talk to the class of 2023?

The fact is these are real feelings that most people experience regardless of gender and many of them will come as a result of the environment around us. They will be affected by our upbringing, parenting styles and how achievements and failures were dealt with growing up as well as the culture of the place we work in. In the main they are normal.

One of the women I spoke to as part of my research for this element of the book was Tara Brevitt. Tara is a former construction project manager, now leadership, business and lifestyle coach, whom I came across on LinkedIn. I was fascinated by Tara's completely different methods of coaching. She's blunt, she swears more than me and she doesn't pussyfoot around, and, to be frank, I really liked that because we all have busy lives and stuff to do!

The biggest thing I liked was her complete belief that imposter syndrome is, in her words, 'BS'. She doesn't believe it's an ever-present 'syndrome', rather that we have inevitable imposter moments. She focuses on coaching people to shift from imposter thought back to reality as quickly as possible. Tara works mostly with women but also some men and works on mindset as she says 'while the environment needs changing we can't always do that but we can change how we feel in that environment'.

She suggests that if we do not feel nerves, excitement, anxiety and fear, it means we are unchallenged and stagnant. She also thinks it's imperative that we get to know who we are and take the time we need to develop ourselves.

Tara says, 'It's not that women need fixing; we don't. But we do need to be authentic and stop exhausting ourselves by trying to be someone else and being so practiced at judgement.' She believes women have been conditioned to be judgemental of others and themselves and that our confidence and happiness become higher if we release ourselves from these behaviours.

Programmes to 'fix' women not the system

There are literally hundreds of programmes that have been produced in an attempt to 'fix' women or make them more like men so that women can advance in the workplace.

If you search the internet for 'women leadership' courses, mentoring programmes or coaching development programmes, you will see hundreds of pages of courses all designed to 'help' women for their next moves into leadership.

The fact is, while many of these programmes can be useful and are designed especially for women, they predominantly work on the premise of women doing things and changing themselves to 'get ahead'.

Women are bombarded with books and articles telling them to network more like men do, or speak up more to get ahead, or get a mentor or a sponsor so they can rise into senior management. Do you see the common theme with all these things? Most work on the assumption that women somehow need 'fixing'.

Women do not need fixing.

Women do not need to be more like men. While they can work on things like confidence or being more assertive or [insert your improvement word here], this does not solve the problem. The problem is the surrounding cultures and systems. I have lost count of the number of times I have been told I should 'be more confident' during my career. The fact is women can have coaching and do a course and come out feeling confident and prepared based on what they have learned, but if they are thrown back into a toxic work situation where poor behaviours, bullying, sexual harassment and gender bias exists, they will not be able to thrive and the course will have been utterly pointless.

What we need is a healthy, safe environment with leaders committed to gender equality, supportive and respectful colleagues, male allies who will call out bad behaviours and workplace practices that support everyone to be themselves.

The 2024 *SDG Gender Index* findings, by Equal Measures 2030, stated that, to create a gender-equal future, everyone needs to act and that widespread systems-level change is required to *fix the system* and not the women![144]

The fact is, as we saw in Chapter 2, when workplaces are safer and provide equality, things are better for everyone. Profit goes up, mental health issues improve and people are happier; everyone rises and this means men also get the benefits of better workplaces and treatment, which is something equally as important considering in UK construction we lose two men every working day to suicide.

The current system damages us all, so let's stop trying to blame women's struggles on women and work together to change the system and the culture so that it's better for all of us.

The 'motherhood penalty'

Women have an additional 'penalty' when it comes to having a career and becoming a mother.

Back in 2015 (updated in 2018), the Department for Business, Innovation and Skills and the Equality and Human Rights Commission commissioned research to investigate pregnancy discrimination.[145] The main findings were that one in nine mothers (11%) reported they had either been dismissed, made redundant or treated so poorly they had to leave their job. Scaled up to the general population that worked out to around 54,000 mothers a year.

One in five mothers said they had experienced harassment or negative comments in respect of pregnancy or flexible working; when scaled up, this worked out to 100,000 mothers a year. Worse, 10% of mothers were discouraged by their employer from attending antenatal appointments, something that is needed to ensure mother and baby are both healthy.

In 2023 it was reported that 250,000 mothers had been forced out of work due to difficulties balancing work and childcare and the research also showed 79% of women reported facing barriers in their career progression due to childcare responsibilities.[146] This can lead to an economic gap, with women leaving the workforce entirely or having to go part time.

Mothers who have two children take home 26% less income than women without children, whereas fathers with at least two children take home 22% more than those without. This inequality worsens over time as well, with the difference in hourly pay between mothers and fathers increasing by almost 30% by the time the child reaches twenty. This loss in lifetime earnings experienced by women raising children is a significant part of the gender pay gap. Why is it fathers' earnings rise but mothers' reduce and why are so many mothers forced out of their jobs?

It is also worth noting that, as a result of these traditional 'gender norms' and biases, men can also feel pressure. They feel pressure to be the primary 'breadwinner', being responsible for the financial stability of the family, and they may suffer as a result of being unable to take time to get to know their children in the early stages as they cannot afford to take time away from work.

When these issues are looked at in tandem they are often referred to as 'the motherhood penalty' and 'the fatherhood forfeit', where women feel they are missing out at work and men feel they are missing out at home. It is not good for anyone, and I will discuss in Chapter 9 some of the things we need to do to improve things for parents.

Pregnant Then Screwed was set up in 2015 by Joeli Brearley, who was sacked two days after telling her employer she was pregnant. The project grew and today it is a charity dedicated to ending the motherhood penalty. They offer support to thousands of women each year and campaign to end the motherhood penalty.[147]

In Chapter 5 we will look at what is happening to women in the industry and particularly at the issue of motherhood. Many women who become mothers are currently treated atrociously by the industry. I hope that we stop using non-disclosure agreements (NDAs) and compromise agreements to hide the systemic abuse of mothers and start treating them with the respect they deserve.

Women's groups?

When I started my career, I was always the only woman. There was no social media or LinkedIn and there were no such things as women's groups that I knew of or could find so I resigned myself to knuckling down and just working hard on my career to get where I wanted to be.

Even when women's groups did become available, I was hesitant to join any for a few reasons:

- I was bullied by girls at both primary and secondary school so was unsure if I could 'trust' women.

- I had been really let down by women I thought were my friends at various times in my life which meant I was quite fearful of other women.

- I had met some women who appeared to be using the groups for the wrong reasons.

- Men I worked with were outright hostile about women-in-construction groups, labelling them as being full of useless women who joined because the only way they were going to get anywhere was by playing the 'woman card' etc, and I didn't want to be judged or have it affect my career prospects.

Then I kept coming across articles that said we should be more like men and network more so eventually I started doing just that. The more I spoke to women in the industry and the more I got to know some of them, the more I realised how important women in construction are and how we can give each other connection, security and support.

There are now various options for women wanting to join groups for support from other women who may have navigated similar issues to them. There are also people helping women in construction to network. For information on specific groups and networks and other ways to connect and get involved, please have a look at the sections on what groups and institutions are doing to improve the industry (Chapter 8) and others to follow/connect with (Chapter 9).

Summary

There are numerous challenges that women face. While they can undertake programmes and have coaching and mentoring to help, the simple fact is that currently there is a systemic problem globally that needs to be fixed in order for women to succeed. It is magnified in the construction industry because women are in the minority (and that's not accounting for other minority groups who are often even more marginalised).

Women and men alike face some of the challenges that women are said to have (eg imposter syndrome, lack of confidence and fear of failure). We need to stop genderising these issues and accept that these feelings can apply to everyone.

Women do suffer from sexual harassment, bullying and harassment in the workplace, as we saw in Chapter 2. We will look in more detail at how this specifically affects women in construction in the next chapter.

Women do have a pay gap in many areas, particularly those who are mothers or carers and take time out from work. These women will often see their career progression held back or stall completely and they can never get that gap back. But men suffer from the fatherhood forfeit.

FIVE
What's Actually Happening For Women In Construction?

In writing this book, I asked difficult questions of women in the industry to enable me to see what has (or has not) changed over the past thirty years, as I knew some women were still dealing with sexism, bullying and harassment and as a result were struggling to achieve what they wanted in their careers. I then wanted to offer tangible ideas of what we can do to improve things for the future.

To identify the issues, I set up an in-depth survey to measure what was happening and how often, and I included specific time-related questions to see, crucially, whether there had been any improvement over time. With some help from Ayo Abbas (a former colleague and amazing marketer), I wrote an invitation to all women in construction and posted it on LinkedIn.[148] Over 500 women responded saying they would like to get involved. Of the 515 women who contacted me, 302 women completed the questionnaire (which had 141 questions in total).

The questionnaire needed tweaking during the first couple of days, as a setting meant every question required completing even if not applicable. Once this was resolved, the data collection process worked as intended. The results enabled me to properly assess the issues women face and, more importantly, see how recently things were happening and whether there had been any improvement over time.

I included some open questions so women could detail specific experiences in their own words. This was particularly important to provide the industry with details of women's lived experience. It also enabled women to provide advice to other women (see Chapter 6); they offer a wealth of advice on the struggles women may face, having navigated similar issues themselves.

Some women contacted me and said it was cathartic completing the questionnaire, while others said it had brought up trauma they had buried and long forgotten. Around 200 women just found it too difficult to complete. The questionnaire did include difficult questions; many required yes/no responses followed by an indication, if they had answered yes, of whether the experience had happened in the last year, last five years, last ten years or longer ago. This was so I could see if things had improved over the last decade and share this information with the industry so we can understand the issues and see what needs to change.

Although I really hoped to see a marked improvement in the types of issues and behaviours women were dealing with today, compared to those I have dealt with in my thirty-year career, I knew from discussions with women prior to starting the book that similar issues were occurring today.

I have spoken to over 1,000 women in construction over the last three years about the various issues they face. In some cases my research has shown there have been improvements in the ways women are treated, which has been refreshing. However, it has also flagged the following as problems that women still face on a daily basis:

- Sexism/harassment
- Bullying
- Bias
- Lack of support from other women
- Pay and promotion struggles
- Issues when returning from childbirth
- Minority women have an added struggle
- Lack of facilities for gender specific needs

In this chapter we will look at some of the statistics from my research and I provide some real examples of things that have happened, and more importantly *still are happening*, to women in the construction industry today.

Sexism and harassment

Sexism and harassment are topics many do not want to talk about. In some cases the issues women face are now so normalised that sexism and harassment either aren't properly discussed or they are outright dismissed as not being an issue at all. But let's be clear, women face it all the time the world over.

Sexism is a form of prejudice, typically against women and girls, and is often linked to power (whereby those with the power are usually treated better than those without, and those without are often discriminated against).

The European Institute for Gender Equality defines sexism as being linked to beliefs about the 'fundamental nature of women and men and the roles they should play in society'.[149] It is often based upon the belief or assumption that one gender (men) is in some way 'superior' to another (women).

In 2020, UN research concluded that, despite decades of progress, *all* of us (nine out of ten people) have some form of ingrained bias towards women and girls, meaning we are all sexist to varying degrees.[150]

The Council of Europe states that sexism in the workplace includes: 'derogatory comments, objectification, sexist humour or jokes, over-familiar remarks, silencing or ignoring people, gratuitous comments about dress and physical appearance, sexist body language, lack of respect and masculine practices which intimidate or exclude women and favour fellow men.'[151]

In a 2017 survey by Hays recruitment firm, 73% of women said they had experienced sexual discrimination, harassment or victimisation. In July 2017 the RICS found that almost one third of women in construction said fear of sexism was holding them back from pursuing senior roles.[152] Sexism harms people and holds them back: it can affect performance, mental health and job satisfaction.

Sexualisation is a particular aspect. The *Sexualisation of Women in the Workplace* research[153] highlighted the scale of sexualisation of women at work and the impact it can have. It found that 55% of women had experienced being sexualised in the workplace and 79% had to adapt their behaviour as a result. It also found 50% had considered leaving their job as a result. This was not a surprise to me as many of the women I have spoken to state categorically that they do not want to be seen in a sexual manner; they want to be respected.

Sexism in construction does contribute to the leaky pipeline we have; after all, if women are not respected and are being bullied, sexualised, harassed or assaulted at work, it's hardly surprising that they leave the industry.

One of my first occasions of being sexually assaulted at work was when a scaffolder accosted me, held me up against a wall and tried to kiss me behind a building in Balham, London. It scared me but I managed to kick him with my steel toe capped boots, and I ran. I didn't tell anyone but knew one of his colleagues saw it. I was later called into the office of my then surveying director, David Lester, as it had been reported; he asked if I was OK and proceeded to ensure that the company removed the scaffolder from the site and from any future site – fabulous leadership many could take note of today!

Sadly, that may have been the first but it certainly wasn't the last incident of sexual harassment or assault I have had in my career. I have had my bum slapped and breasts squeezed, and I have been groped and forcefully kissed, as well as being the victim of two far more serious sexual assaults that, in hindsight now, I wish I had felt strong enough to report to the police. I didn't because I was scared that:

- I would not be taken seriously
- I'd somehow lose my job despite the fact I had done nothing wrong

The only times I made formal reports, I (like many of the women I have spoken to through the course of researching this book) was the one to suffer. The first was a report about a client who kept hitting on me during meetings and the second was due to a colleague who sexually harassed me and scared the life out of me.

On the 'client' issue I was not supported by the company; instead I was made to feel like it was somehow my fault and told I couldn't do my job if I could not be alone with the sleazy client. There was no concern for my safety and things went downhill pretty fast for my career in that company.

The second issue was where I had reported the unwanted sexual advances of a colleague and, again, it was not taken seriously. I was forced to continue working with him and the stress affected my health and made me ill; I became a statistic, another woman forced into a compromise agreement. This happened the morning I returned to work after three months' sick leave for treatment for CIN3 high grade pre-malignant cervical cancer, picked up on a routine smear test. (Please, anyone with a womb reading this book, ensure you have your regular smear tests – they may not be pleasant but they could save your life.) I was greeted with the MD and HR walking towards me saying we needed to talk, only to be told they wanted me gone, whereas the colleague who assaulted me kept his job and his career and continued to flourish at that company.

I hoped things had changed but my research showed women continue to face sexism, harassment and sexual assault in the workplace.

We looked at sexual harassment in Chapter 2 but sexual assault is different. In the UK, the Sexual Offences Act 2023, Section 3 describes sexual assault in the following way:[154]

(1) A person (A) commits an offence if—
   (a) he intentionally touches another person (B),
   (b) the touching is sexual,
   (c) B does not consent to the touching, and
   (d) A does not reasonably believe that B consents.

(2) Whether a belief is reasonable is to be determined having regard to all the

circumstances, including any steps A has taken to ascertain whether B consents.

The question I asked women in my survey was:

Have you ever been touched inappropriately (sexual assault) by a colleague/client/subcontractor or supplier in the workplace or on site?

Of the 302 women surveyed, 92 women said they had been sexually assaulted at work at some point in their career: a huge 30.46%.

However, I wanted to see if things had improved so I then asked a second question aimed at determining when this had occurred and this showed that sixteen women had been sexually assaulted at work in the last year:

If you have been touched inappropriately in the workplace or on site, when did this happen?

Timeframe	Response	%
In the last year	16	17.39%
In the last 1 to 5 years	17	18.48%
In the last 5 to 10 years	26	28.26%
Over 10 years ago	33	35.87%
Total	92	100%

Using this data I then calculated the ratio of women this has happened to enable me to see the change up or down:

Ratio of women assaulted

Timeframe	Ratio	Ratio expressed (no of women in 10)
In the last year	1.74:10	2 in every 10 women
In the last 10 years	**3.05:10**	**3 in every 10 women**

It is evident that, based on the women I surveyed, the rates of sexual assault have reduced over time. However, this isn't a minor issue: this is sexual assault of women at work, and my research shows that still in 2022/2023 **two in ten of the women I surveyed who had been sexually assaulted at work had experienced this in the last year**.

In September 2024 the BBC released an article confirming women in skilled trades were being subjected to 'appalling' levels of sexism according to workers and new research.[155]

Some of the things happening to women in construction are harrowing, but we need to stop hiding these experiences so that we can stop the abuse. Here are a few of the things women told me have happened to them in the workplace in the last few years:

'As a sixteen- to eighteen-year-old apprentice electrician on site it was awful. My bum was slapped every time I was up a ladder, breasts groped once by an older colleague and then at electrical college on the college bus I was constantly having verbal sexual abuse from all the boys on my course.' (Electrician)

'I was pushed up against a wall by a male colleague on site and I could feel his erection through his trousers (I didn't feel I could tell anyone, like it was my fault).' (Quantity Surveyor)

'My manager used to sit next to me at my desk and put his hand on my thigh and tell me not to tell anyone.' (Quantity Surveyor)

There were worse experiences. One woman, whom I spoke to in more depth after reading her responses, said she was on a work night out, the only female with around twelve men:

'... and a much older colleague was "helping me get back to the hotel". I had drunk too much and was emotional after a relationship breakdown. I don't remember getting back but I vaguely remember pushing him away as he tried to kiss me. The next thing I remember was waking up and I was on the bed and he was on top of me, his hand was in my underwear and his fingers inside me, his trousers were down. I said no and tried to push him away and he acted casual and stopped, pulled back his cock hanging out and pulled his bottoms up and left. I have never got over it and always blamed myself as I'd had too much to drink. I almost got raped.' (Quantity Surveyor)

WHAT'S ACTUALLY HAPPENING FOR WOMEN?

Have things changed? More recently women have said the following:

> 'My colleague made sexual innuendo all the time. I was brave and reported to his director, but his director downplayed it. Then on a company dinner, night out, the director I reported it to tried to kiss me in the lift, when we were alone, and when I pushed him off, he said he was just checking if I was "easy". I resigned the next day.' (Designer)

> 'A male boss was undoubtedly sexually discriminating against me and was sexist. That I did report and had absolutely no support from the female HR manager.' (Design Consultant)

> 'Constant verbal sexual harassment then unfair dismissal after reporting.' (Construction Manager)

There are also things that women may do to try and fit in as there is so much pressure on them. I myself did it, not only with the things I wore (manly suits and shirts) and my mannerisms but also around things like trying to fit in with the drinking culture. This can make things even worse.

In November 2023 I was interviewed for an article about drinking in the construction industry.[156] Back when I started, drinking was par for the course and often done to excess. I drank, sometimes to excess; I stayed out late, going home drunk; and I went to the late-night lap dancing clubs with the men I worked with in my attempts to be seen as part of the 'team' and not as the outsider. As I learned over the years, though, these actions can also put you at risk, particularly if you are a woman, often in the minority or the only woman on nights out.

In the article about drinking, a woman had come forward and shared her story about a work night out where drink had no doubt played a part in an attempted sexual assault by her drunken colleague. The thing that had upset her most was the fact that, despite reporting it, her company had not supported her; in fact they appeared to support the colleague by simply saying sorry with flowers, thinking that would be an acceptable end to the issue. I tracked her down and we spoke about the impact these events had on her. She said:

> 'It was bad enough that I felt stupid for opening my hotel room door that night in the first place (something I would never do now), which led to the project manager (who I thought was a friend) launching himself on me. But the worst thing was that he and the company thought a bunch of flowers and a sorry would make it OK. They forced me to continue working with him even though I told them I did not feel safe, and they supported him, the man, just to get the project done using that as an excuse.
>
> 'They then went on a mission to destroy me, yet he was rewarded with promotions and kudos. I was treated abysmally, and they

know it was me who made that report to the journalist as two of the directors involved at that time looked me up on LinkedIn the day that article came out and they aren't connected to me. Those men all rallied together and protected another man rather than protecting the woman who was attacked. It's sick and shows the culture we deal with in this industry. Women are considered expendable and if you speak out your life is made absolute hell and your career can end up in tatters along with your mental and physical health. That company broke me, and I hope all of them involved read this and feel sick at the way they treated me because they all know what they did.'

Is this what we want for women? That they suffer reprisals if they report something or are forced out of jobs and left unsupported or are still traumatised years later by the lack of respect and support shown to them?

Sadly, the statistics show this isn't a one-off occurrence. I asked the women I surveyed the following question:

Have you ever been touched inappropriately on work 'nights out' or 'events' by colleagues/ subcontractors/suppliers or clients?

Of the 302 women I surveyed, 98 (32%) said yes, they had been, and 22 of these said it had happened in the last year! That means two in ten women who had been sexually assaulted on work nights out/events by colleagues, clients, suppliers or subcontractors had experienced this in the previous year.

In 2023, Crest Nicholson was found liable for a rape committed after its 2019 Christmas party by a site manager it employed.[157] The most concerning issue was that the site manager concerned had already been witnessed sexually assaulting another woman colleague at the same party and no one had done anything.

It's not just about drink and it's not just in the UK either; sexism, harassment and assaults happen globally in construction. A construction manager from the US told her story of sexism and the fact that 'I don't wear low-cut shirts or anything that would draw attention to my body. Even in baggy pants and boots, I've gotten hit on, and guys on the job site will stare at me as I walk by. Some make it obvious. Others, you could just feel them watching you. It used to make me uncomfortable, but I eventually got used to it.'[158]

Should women really have to deal with this behaviour and just 'get used to it'? I knew I had altered my behaviour at work in the past to deal with some of the issues I faced so in my research I asked women if they had ever worn a 'facade' at work and a massive 58% of women said yes, they did. Women should be able to be themselves, but it is evident that many women simply can't be and will change things about themselves to try and 'fit in' and/or 'protect themselves'.

As noted in Chapter 3, 78% of tradeswomen said they had previously witnessed or experienced discrimination against women and 5.88% had directly experienced sexual assault.[159] The issues can be more pronounced for women in trade positions, particularly those who may be in lone working positions like crane operators.

I spoke to three women who are crane operators (two in the UK and one in the US) and all had been abused and sexually harassed.

One had been stalked so badly by a colleague she had had to leave her job and use her union to take her employer through the unfair dismissal process as her employer refused to sack the man she'd reported to the police (who was often hiding in the yard and waiting for her at 4am when she went to collect her crane for the day and was also stalking her outside of work), meaning she had to find a new job for her own safety.

One had left her job due to the fact she was not only dealing with sexist comments and abuse about being a woman crane driver but also being put under immense pressure to work through lunch breaks and stay working often beyond 7pm (having started her day at 4.30am), meaning the lack of flexibility gave her no life and no chance to see her family. She was, in her words, 'treated like a number not a human'.

Lastly there was a mobile crane operator and photographer I spoke to in the US after seeing her LinkedIn post about not getting a job due to the fact it was known she had refused to be blackmailed into having sex with a foreman on a site she was working on some years before.[160]

Then there's the woman consultant I spoke to a week before finishing this book. A colleague engineer got into a taxi with her so he could 'drop her safely home' after a work event but then forced his way into her home to try and assault her; the next day at work he pretended nothing had happened.

These issues are horrifying and sadly not one-offs.

Bullying

Bullying is another issue many women face, and this section is about its prevalence and the effect bullying has on women in construction.

I want to make it clear here that I am not detracting from men. I recognise, having spoken to many men during my research for the book, that men also suffer from bullying and issues with the culture in the industry. We only have to look at the statistics of losing two men every working day to suicide in UK construction to see things need to improve for men too, but for now let's concentrate on the issues women are facing and the results of my research as it is my firm belief that if we tackle the issues that keep women out of the industry or lead to them leaving we can improve things for everyone.

Bullying and harassment are significant workplace issues and behaviours can range from unwelcome comments or remarks and persistent criticism to unwanted physical contact and shouting.

The Cambridge Dictionary describes a bully as 'someone who hurts or frightens someone else, often over a period of time, and often forcing them to do something that they do not want to do'.[161]

There is currently no legal definition of bullying in the UK, but the UK Government describes bullying and harassment as behaviour that makes someone feel intimidated or offended and gives examples of behaviours such as:

- Spreading malicious rumours
- Unfair treatment
- Picking on or regularly undermining someone
- Denying someone's training or promotion opportunities.[162]

Bullying and harassment can occur in numerous ways (in person, by phone, by letter, by email and nowadays also on social media) and, while bullying is not against the law in the UK, harassment *is* unlawful. Harassment is defined as *unwanted behaviour* that has the purpose or effect of violating a person's dignity, or of creating an intimidating, hostile, degrading, humiliating or offensive environment for the person, and the behaviour is related to one of the following:[163]

- Age
- Sex
- Disability

- Gender reassignment
- Marriage and civil partnership
- Pregnancy and maternity
- Race
- Religion or belief
- Sexual orientation

Some of us may think back to bullying at school, and when we leave school we perhaps naively believe that bullying is behind us. Sadly, that is often not the case, particularly for women and other minorities as they often continue to encounter bullying and harassment at work.

I have been bullied a number of times during my thirty-year career and I know from personal experience the toll it can take. I remember one of my first experiences on site as an eighteen-year-old trainee quantity surveyor measuring head restraints, where I didn't make it far before a man told me I was a C*** and I should F*** off back to the kitchen as I didn't belong on site.

I have been shouted at in front of people on sites by subcontractors and managers, particularly in the early years of my career working for different contractors when things were more antiquated than they are now. I was also regularly shouted at by a director who also had a habit of throwing phones and pens around the office when he didn't like something.

It made me deeply unhappy, and sometimes I dreaded work. I felt sick and remember in one job I would start to feel anxiety on a Sunday thinking of going to work the next day. Sometimes I tried to shrug it off, sometimes I stayed silent and simply found another job, worried that if I spoke up it would affect my career, but each time it affected my health mentally and physically.

My fear of the consequences for my career meant that I have never reported bullying. Most of the time I just found another job and left or tried to stay away from the person doing the bullying.

Some types of bullying can be more covert and harder to deal with as they are almost impossible for people outside the interpersonal interaction to see. These can be things like exclusion tactics, maybe not being invited to something everyone else was or not being given the same opportunities as others; being ignored and having people act like you aren't there or having people talking over you or about you while in earshot; nasty comments or jokes that are hard to deal with and will often be denied by a person who will claim 'it was just a joke' or they were 'just having fun'.

There can be changes in tone or behaviours towards you. I remember being told by a man, who sat and folded his arms when I asked an innocent question, 'I don't have to explain myself to you, you should just do as I say' (suggesting that as a woman I'm inferior, so how dare I ask a question).

Even more recently following major anterior spinal fusion surgery in January 2019, after six months of not travelling while waiting for my bones to fuse, I was verbally abused on my first outing to a seminar by a former colleague. He walked towards me at lunchtime and I was completely unprepared when he said, 'Oh my god, what happened to you? You've got really fat. You used to be the most glamorous woman I knew.' My confidence, suffice to say, hit rock bottom and I left the seminar in tears.

Bullying is a huge issue for women in the industry and it can be even tougher for women in trades. GMB Union's study in 2021 (which found only 3% of blue collar construction workers are women) concluded that the industry 'must end the disgraceful environment women are subjected to on the shop floor.'[164] The same year, a survey of mental health in the industry conducted by Herts Tools found that one in four people had been bullied in the workplace and this had a direct impact on their mental health and productivity.[165]

If we want more women in the industry we have to improve the culture both on- and off-site for everyone.

I have spoken to many women in construction over the years and it was clear many had suffered. A staggering 62% of the women I surveyed said they had been bullied in the workplace.

While we have to acknowledge there are people out there who intentionally set out to bully others I am a firm believer that most people don't wake up in the morning and think 'I'm going to be an awful person and make someone's life miserable today'.

Some people may not realise what they are doing or saying is harming another person. Banter, jokes or sarcastic comments can be harmful to the person on the receiving end and 28% of employees have said that 'banter' is often used as an excuse when someone raises the fact they are upset.[166] 'It was only a joke' – we've all heard that one, haven't we?

I asked the women I spoke to and surveyed to provide examples and they ranged from women still being shouted at and abused by men (and yes, this is happening even now in 2024 as I write this) to email bullying, social media bullying and bullying by other women, which we will look at in the next section.

I have put a few examples below just to give you a chance to see what women are dealing with daily in construction:

'Abusive and threatening language when out on site.' (Quantity Surveyor)

'Bullied by a senior manager for no apparent reason. Would berate me in the open office in front of the team, very patronising and condescending. Ended up moving to another part of the office or working at home to get away. Ended up being scored lower on my appraisal as I "didn't handle situation appropriately", despite reporting to manager and HR. Ended up leaving the company.' (Project Manager)

'This happened recently with [a large Tier 1 firm]. Bullying, toxic work environment, inappropriate

> racist comments made by a director to me, he said the C word in the office. For the first time in my career, I raised a grievance. This encouraged five other people to (I came into the office and it had been going for months, to the knowledge of senior management but they did nothing). I never heard the outcome of my grievance. They moved me to another project on the other side of the country (away from my support network) and promoted the male to the leadership board. I escalated this to the exec board and met with them in London. They made excuses. These companies are all lip service and don't care.' (Commercial Manager)

> 'MD was openly aggressive to me in front of the entire office for correcting him on something – he thumped his fist on my desk. In my view he would have never behaved so aggressively to a male colleague. I handed in my notice.' (Engineer)

> 'Male verbal bullying in person and over Teams – aggressive tones, passive aggressive attitude and patronising behaviour towards my abilities and my work. Felt very devalued, low and depressed which would come and go. A bit like domestic violence in the sense that the misbehaviour would be "rectified" (in their eyes) by equally nice behaviour.' (Quantity Surveyor)

This last one was a common theme in the responses, ie men who will bully or be nasty and then flip and act the complete opposite way and think everything is OK because they are now being nice.

The term 'gaslighting' comes to mind when I read some of the experiences women reported and even I have had it where a senior person seeks to minimise their own awful behaviour by saying things like 'it was just a joke' or 'you're too sensitive' or tries to invalidate your feelings when you tell them you feel devalued or disrespected by making it all about them, with phrases like 'I take offence at that, I've done XYZ for you', and then flipping the conversation to suit them.

This is not normal behaviour, yet it is commonplace and while it continues women (and others) in the industry suffer.

Then we have the bullies that try to turn it on the victim or say overly personal things that are likely to deeply offend:

'I recorded the various things which were said and first challenged the individual saying it was unacceptable and unprofessional. The only response from him was, "Oh, are you going to try and report me for bullying? That won't look very good on you, will it."' (Project Director)

'The director chose to pick on my weight, my work production, my overall clothing and dress sense. It was endless. Not only affected my mental health but also my physical health.' (Engineer)

> 'Since being a quantity surveyor on my last scheme I was bullied by the groundwork subcontractor, I question whether the way they spoke and dealt with me would have been the same if I was male.' (Quantity Surveyor)

> 'I have been verbally and physically attacked on site and lied to/bullied at director level.' (Project Manager)

Of the 188 women (of 302 surveyed) who said they had been bullied, 113 (60%) said they had formally reported the bullying, 73 said they had not reported and 2 said not applicable.

Sadly, 59% of those who reported bullying said it had not been taken seriously and 76 of them (67%) said they had received no support and 67 of them (59%) said the company didn't even investigate the issue.

> 'It has happened pretty much constantly. I can hold my own against bullies, but I am fed up of organisations who protect them for their perceived value.' (Designer)

This shows us that women are not valued and are not being taken seriously. Women need to be supported. Is it any wonder that we have the 'leaky pipeline'?

I then asked the women who didn't report the bullying why they hadn't done so. Here are a few of the responses:

'I didn't feel anyone would believe me and also I loved being an apprentice, so I didn't want to lose the opportunity to finish the course.' (Cost Consultant)

'I knew I wouldn't get support from senior management or HR.' (Director)

'I have also experienced issues in the last eight years in my current company. Sometimes this has been brushed under the carpet or only partially dealt with (ie that person eventually left). It is a sensitive topic for any business and lots of leadership teams turn a blind eye to emotional workplace bullying.' (Architect)

'The person that was bullying was the director and owner of the company, so I didn't have anyone to report to.' (Engineer)

'Because experience has taught me that reporting things just makes you (as a female) more of an outsider and gives you a bad reputation.' (Commercial Manager)

'As I knew nothing would be done about it and it could potentially lead to being pushed out the door.' (Project Manager)

'It would have ended my career.' (Construction Manager)

'Because most times, you are better to go somewhere else with the chance of working with decent people than spend time fighting it. Although sometimes you have to stand up for yourself and fight it for your own mental health first. Nothing worse than injustice.' (Quantity Surveyor)

'I knew it would be held against me, as if I couldn't manage my role.' (Site Manager)

'I didn't feel I would be supported.' (Designer)

The fact is, as a woman in the industry none of this surprises me, as it echoes my own experience. I know bullying happens to men as well as women but women are still very much in the minority, so it has a bigger impact if women leave the industry as a result.

If we are to improve the situation for women we need to improve the culture to ensure we do not have 62% of women trying to navigate a career in the industry while being bullied.

We need a zero-tolerance culture for bullying so we do not have so many women being pushed out of their job when they do report it or alternatively being too scared to report it because they fear their career will be over or they will get no support.

The fact that 70% of the women who said they had reported bullying said they had been made to feel they were being too emotional or sensitive reiterates the toxic culture women have to navigate when these situations occur.

People have a right to be treated with dignity and respect at work and organisations need to start taking the issue seriously. Bullying is damaging and, for the industry to become more inclusive and improve mental health for everyone, it's an issue that needs to be addressed.

Women who are hard on other women

Ever heard that phrase 'there's a place in hell for women who don't support other women'? Well I am now going to be controversial because I do not agree with it as a blanket term.

I will always support women who are working hard and striving to achieve *but* not at any cost. If a woman doesn't live by my values, is dishonest or is out to hurt others then why should I support her just because we are the same gender?

However, when it comes to women who do not support other women when it's unrelated to a clash in values or dishonesty, what is the problem?

Many of us may have heard of 'Queen Bee' syndrome. This is when women behave in typically male ways to fit in (so they may display more 'male' characteristics like assertiveness and confidence as opposed to more 'female' traits like empathy and interpersonal relationship building). This is in part because some women at the top are there because they have convinced men that they are not like other women. This behaviour was recognised by Gill Whitty-Collins in her research where some of the women found to be winning at work were doing so because they behave like men (referred to as 'Manly Ones').[167]

Then there is the invisible law in female culture called 'The Power Dead Rule', coined by Pat Heim and colleagues in the book *Hardball for Women*.[168] This rule governs relationships and self-esteem and for women assumes that the self-esteem and power must be similar in weight for women, ie 'dead-even'. Where it differs and the power balance is disrupted, for example where a woman rises in status above other women, the result may be that women ostracise her, talk behind her back or belittle her. This is often a subconscious process.

This links to 'Tall Poppy Syndrome', another social phenomenon where people are resented, excluded or criticised for their success and merit; rather than someone's achievements being celebrated, that person is cut down and subconsciously relegated, meaning their successes and accomplishments are often under attack. While this is not just about women, research has shown that women and people of colour are affected more than others in the workplace and the more accomplished a woman is, the more likely it is she will face aggressions like bullying, belittling and challenges to her success, not only from those in senior positions, but also from her peers.[169]

I recently learned about white women who are unsupportive and sometimes feel threatened by women from different ethnic groups and I know Anita

Phagura is currently undertaking research on this particular issue, which I look forward to reading.[170]

There are also women who don't support other women because there are very few women in the group/company or industry, meaning they feel threatened when another woman comes along, or women who may have struggled to reach their position, overcoming various obstacles, and, as a result, they have a battle-worn attitude to other women where they think 'I had to struggle, you should too'.

Women in the workplace who may be unsupportive and sometimes outright aggressive to other women can be difficult. When I started my survey, various men I know in construction shared my post and questionnaire with their networks and I immediately had this response from a woman in the industry:

> 'There is nothing more frustrating than separating women from men and suggesting that there is a difference. Moreover, the more you talk about the difference, the worse it is… If you want to help, stop this nonsense campaign and better start improving schools. There is the origin of your problem.'

I have not included the entire quote as some of it was rather scathing of the UK, but it's a perfect example of a woman who had seemingly done OK in her career and as a result could not see any other viewpoint and did not want to 'be involved' in helping to measure progress (even if she had had positive experiences), and seemingly was unable to empathise with women who may have struggled.

Of the 302 women who responded to my survey, 217 said they had at some point had a woman boss/authority figure, and over 50% (116) of these said they had experienced a woman boss/authority figure being unsupportive to them. There were varying reasons ranging from competition, jealousy, being hardened from the environment, feeling threatened by other women to them being insecure in themselves and projecting that onto others. I have included some of the comments to demonstrate that the issues in the industry are not solely related to men – we definitely have issues with some women too:

> 'My female manager was horrible when I first started at the construction firm. She would blame me for anything that happened, things that were completely out of my control, for example, when consultants missed deadlines, this was my fault.'

> 'I have been bullied twice, both times by women bosses.'

> 'The worst bullying I have ever encountered has unfortunately been at the hands of a woman with more experience than me, and in a C-suite position. She actively seeks to undermine me and exclude me from work, and has been rude/dismissive on numerous occasions.'

'This has happened twice and been by women who have disliked having female competition. The first time I was misled about procedure by a woman who "took me under her wing" so I would make mistakes and get told off by the boss. She also used to imply that I was having an affair with a man in a meeting where it was just her, me and twenty-five men on a weekly basis and suggest I sat on his knee or ask why I didn't want to when everyone knew we were at it like rabbits. We were both married and I hardly knew him. He was always very supportive about it and I think he wasn't as embarrassed as me but he could see how much it affected me. When I reported it, I was moved. Another woman appeared to want to be close friends but then would share all the details of my personal life with people in the office in a negative way. Because the men in the office were more discreet, I didn't know she was saying these things for months and shared quite a few things that I would never have shared with a wider audience. When I reported it, the reply was that it was "just Kate" and that I shouldn't be so sensitive.'

'I was bullied by a female director, they shouted at me in the open office, would ring me on my days off and late in the evenings demanding work was done.'

'It has always been women that have made my work life a misery, not men. I think being in a male dominated environment sometimes pushes the few women apart because there is a sense of competition.'

While this book is about women and making things better for them, we also have to acknowledge that some women go out of their way to hurt or bully other women. We have to call this behaviour out as much as we should be calling out bullying and bad behaviour from men.

Pay and promotion struggles

We all know about the gender pay gap discussed in Chapter 2 but what are women in the construction industry actually dealing with?

I know throughout my career there have been numerous times I have found out men were earning more than me. The first time this happened I was in my early twenties and the difference between me and a male colleague turned out to be £10k. When I brought this up to my then surveying director and was asked what I expected him to do about it, I said pay us the same of course. His reply was 'that's not going to happen', so I (having gone in prepared for this eventuality) simply placed my resignation on the desk and walked out of his office. I took a job with a specialist contractor and bagged myself an £11k increase.

In 2022 Rated People research found that women in fifteen key trades in the industry earned just 72% of what men did. The biggest gap was between women and male electricians where women earned just 54% of what men did.[171]

It's not just seen in trade roles either. In 2023, research by *New Civil Engineer* and *Construction News* revealed women occupied less than 10% of the top-paying jobs at the biggest contractors. When it came to the gender pay gap, the biggest hourly gap was seen at Costain Limited with a median gap between men and women at a huge 30.4% while the smallest gap was at Laing O'Rourke with a 3.9% difference.[172]

In my research I asked the question:

Have you ever found out a male colleague was earning more than you for doing the same role?

I wasn't remotely surprised when of the 302 women a whopping 63.58% answered yes. When I asked what they had done as a result many said they had simply left the company. Others said they felt too intimidated to bring up the issue and some said there was no point discussing it as they knew they would be bullied or pushed out. Here are a few of the comments women gave, all of which demonstrate why we have retention issues and often lose women either from companies or from the industry as a whole:

'I told my line manager that I had found out what salary this particular person was on, and I asked to be matched (I should've asked for more, but I didn't) seeing as we started at the same time, were equally academically qualified yet I had more health and safety experience than him. They gave me a £1,500 pay rise, which was still £5,500 less than him. I left the organisation within the next six months.' (H&S Professional)

'I asked for a raise and was ignored.' (Quantity Surveyor)

'I received an unsatisfactory response and chose to leave the company.' (Project Manager)

'Raised this and once again, brushed off. This happened recently with [a large Tier 1 firm] and I escalated it to senior management and HR. I was promised a review. I chased constantly; nothing happened. They claimed I was getting paid the proper range for my experience. Funnily in my next role, I went straight to Executive Director and was promoted again within three months to Senior Exec Director.' (Project Manager)

'I got a new employer and left.' (Quantity Surveyor)

'I complained and was told earnings were a private matter and I should not have that information.' (Designer)

When it came to promotion things are equally as frustrating, over 42% of the women I surveyed (128 of the 302 surveyed) said they had left their job as they did not feel they were getting the same promotional opportunities men were. Some women didn't mention it and the comments as to why were concerning, saying things like:

'I didn't mention it, because what's the point? It would be considered making trouble, and I often feel exhausted from constantly sticking my head above the parapet anyway.' (Quantity Surveyor)

Those who raised the issue with their employer (and many didn't – they simply quit) were often greeted with responses that show a disregard for women and their potential when it comes to promotion:

'I was strung along for nearly three years saying they would promote me to Design Manager (DM) but they never did, even when I got my MCIOB. I was doing the role of DM but getting paid as a Design Coordinator (DC). When I side-stepped into a Sustainability role because of my skills and self-learning in the area (no pay increase, mind), they promoted two men to DM who had not been there as long as I had, one of which I'd even trained up on a few things. I eventually got fed up of being taken for granted and moved companies.' (Designer)

'Recently interviewed for a internal promotion role, I felt that my experience was valued less than the successful candidate (a man) from the feedback that I received after the interview.' (Engineer)

'I was told I was lucky to be in my position as a woman and not to go for promotion.' (Quantity Surveyor)

'I raised them [my concerns] and was told I couldn't handle it… I left that employer.' (Site Manager)

> 'Yes – A graduate with less experience was promoted to associate on completing their training. I had significantly more experience and had been promised the promotion. I received an unsatisfactory response and chose to leave the company rather than have the partners believe I accepted the situation.' (Project Manager)

One of the most shocking comments on this issue was from a quantity surveyor:

> 'They stated that due to being on maternity leave for one year it wasn't fair for me to have a promotion as I hadn't been working for the last year – they used that excuse for two years until I left.'

This is just a small selection of the comments women provided and it sadly shows the ongoing theme of women not being taken as seriously as men and not being promoted even when they have the necessary experience.

Motherhood and minorities in construction – the additional gap

Women can be held back for a number of reasons, but the motherhood gap is something that cannot be ignored. Of the women I surveyed, 45% thought they had been discriminated against because they were a woman of childbearing age.

WHAT'S ACTUALLY HAPPENING FOR WOMEN?

I remember earlier in my career being asked outright at interviews if I planned on having children. I have also had discussions with directors in the past who thought the gender pay gap was OK because women 'go and have a "year off" each time they have a baby'.

While asking these types of questions and discriminating against mothers is illegal, it still happens. In my research, 144 of the 302 women I surveyed said they were mothers and over half of them (76) said they thought they had been discriminated against since becoming a mother and the same number said they'd been treated differently at work since becoming a mother.

When I asked if they had been discriminated against in terms of promotional prospects since becoming a mother, 57% of the 144 mothers said they had, and the same percentage said they had lost out on pay rises and bonuses since becoming a mother.

Careers After Babies research in 2023 found 98% of women want to return to work but of those who go back full time 57% leave within two years, many as a result of redundancy or ill mental health.[173] It also found that when women get put in different roles after maternity leave, 79% of women leave within two years.

This treatment of women and the struggles they face pre- and post-motherhood is echoed in my research. Here are just a few of the comments women have given me in respect of how they have been treated as expectant mothers, adoptive mothers and returning mothers. These women range from quantity surveyors and designers to project managers and tradeswomen and almost all mothers who completed my survey are suffering.

> 'I have been bullied at my current company as a pregnant female by the general manager and one of the directors, since notifying them of my pregnancy. They only communicate with me via email (prior to this there was banter and a lot of casual meetings to confirm/organise things).'

> 'I was bullied to consider an early return from maternity leave, because according to the practice I was in a senior position.'

> 'I felt bullied during a pregnancy.'

> 'Line manager refused to return me to job after maternity leave.'

> 'While our company provides reasonable flexibility, the undercurrent is that you cannot be a mother and be a leader.'

> 'When I returned from maternity leave ten weeks after having my child the MD had accidentally given me access to a new organisation chart where I had been demoted two levels below my role prior to maternity leave, with a new employee in my old role as head of department – I had to show him how I did my job on

> my first day back which happened to be his first day. The company said ... we didn't expect you to come back after you had the baby.'

> 'My experience might suggest that working mothers who work part time are first to be made redundant during a consultation phase.'

> 'It was clear that I could not have maternity leave, so I had no time off to have my daughter.'

While we allow companies to treat pregnant women and returning mothers this way, we will continue to lose women in the industry. However, UK legislation doesn't help. Parental leave pay in the UK is the lowest in Europe.

Things have to change. Women who become mothers should not be losing out on promotions or being forced to leave companies because they request flexibility. Nine women I spoke to in 2024 and twelve in 2023 had become mothers and had then been forced into redundancy or put on compromise agreements when they asked for more flexibility – and some of them worked for big contractors. While becoming a mother is no doubt life changing, being a mother does not mean women are less capable.

One of the things I realised prior to embarking on writing this book was that while women face gender bias, the situation gets worse for ethnic women as they have an additional race bias that I as a white woman do not have.

I first realised this when I was having conversations with women who were speaking on a panel with me. I was shocked by the additional struggles they were having due to being non-white women, with some of them facing outright racism at work on top of the everyday sexism women often deal with.

In 2022, lived experience research undertaken by four organisations looked at issues around inclusive workplaces and found experiences are worse for those in other marginalised groups, particularly around ethnicity, and that women in this group suffered from the 'double whammy' of being both a woman and being non-white.[174]

One of the women I spoke to during my research, a senior black woman working in the consulting side of the industry, said, 'I always stood out as a woman of colour and had to work harder and cope with racial discrimination and I didn't complain as I had to work so hard to get to where I was I didn't want to risk being the difficult black woman and ruining all my hard work.'

Women should not be suffering due to gender, motherhood or ethnicity; we must change the culture and ensure this discrimination stops.

PPE for women

Part of making the industry more inclusive means going back to basics. How can women feel included if they cannot find PPE that fits them correctly and allows them to do their jobs safely?

The lack of PPE that fits women (and some smaller framed men) is something that has dogged the industry for years. My first experience of drowning in ill-fitting 'unisex' PPE was back in the early 1990s when the smallest jackets and vests for my then tiny size 8 frame quite simply drowned me. The boots in a size 6 were a nightmare to source (I actually procured my first pair myself as my employer's supplier simply did not go down that small) and I got used to tripping up in my ill-fitting heavy boots that needed extra socks and still rubbed, getting snagged on door handles and scaffolding due to over-sized jackets with sleeves too long and vests too baggy and, when gloves and glasses were introduced, having to constantly push the glasses up while struggling to write or hold handrails as the gloves even in extra small were still too big for my hands.

Caroline Criado-Perez wrote about the fact PPE is designed around the sizes and characteristics of male populations in Europe and the US in her book *Invisible Women*. It is unsurprising, if its design is based on the male population, that it fails to adequately fit or protect women, who are a completely different body shape and size.[175]

It's not just the UK and the US either.[176] In Canada a survey of 3,000 women in 2022 found that 50% said their PPE did not fit properly, 43% said it was uncomfortable and 38% said women-specific PPE was inadequate.[177]

In 2016 Prospect Union published a report where of the respondents they surveyed only 17% of women in construction currently wore PPE designed for women.

As I write this in 2023/2024, there are people like Katherine Evans – winner of the *Construction News* and *New Civil Engineer* award for 'Women's Network of the Year 2023' and winner of 'Local Hero and Most Influential Overall 2024' at the CITB and National Federation of Builders Top 100 Women in Construction Awards – and Katy Robinson – a senior project manager at East Riding of Yorkshire Council and campaign manager for the National Association of Women in Construction (Yorkshire region) – pushing for change, as well as people like Leena Begum, who challenged inclusivity and won an award for her work on a range of PPE for Muslim women.[178]

Evans wrote an article about the PPE issue and even reading the comments after the article it is evident how big the issue is for women and how some men would prefer to victim blame women rather than work towards getting them (and other men who do not fit the average stereotyped male PPE fit) the right equipment to do their job safely.[179] Katherine has trialled and tested with her Bold as Brass members various types of PPE designed specifically for women and she is now a dear friend of mine. I am so proud of the work she has done improving PPE for women and other minority groups.

The fact is the lack of properly fitting PPE for women has always been a health and safety matter that puts women's lives at risk. Women are not scaled down versions of men; we generally have shorter

WHAT'S ACTUALLY HAPPENING FOR WOMEN?

torsos and legs than men but have wider hips and chests, yet here we are thirty years later and only now, after years of struggle, is the issue being treated with the seriousness it deserves. However, it is evident there is a general lack of awareness as to what PPE is out there that is properly designed for women and moreover there can still be a 'money' issue where procurement is still around bulk buying and the cheapest 'unisex' option rather than ensuring PPE is 'personal' to the user.

The CIOB recently (with the help of some vocal women in the industry like Evans with the PPE Revolution Campaign) have been driving awareness of the lack of inclusive PPE in the industry, yet still I have spoken to women while writing this book who say they ask for women-specific PPE and the quantity surveyor or procurement team questions the price.[180]

The issues for women go further than just ill-fitting PPE; it goes into the entire welfare issue. Toilets are another great example of a seemingly simple issue that just should not be happening in 2024. Many times there are issues with non-male toilets being locked and women workers or visitors needing to go and 'request the key' from someone or, the only woman on site (yes that was often me) being the key holder to protect said toilet from being used as a store room or ending up unhygienic from abuse by others.

I even remember having to fight a well-known contractor not that many years ago to get a sanitary bin put in the toilet on one site I worked on – I was seriously asked why I needed one and looked at as though I was completely mad to be asking for it.

The Construction (Design and Management) Regulations 2015, Schedule 2 still simply states '1.—(1) Suitable and sufficient sanitary conveniences must be provided or made available at readily accessible places'.[181] Why, when we know many working women have a monthly cycle and some people may suffer from other issues needing sanitary disposal equipment, would you not provide the necessary welfare facilities for it as standard? It took the HSE until 2022 to issue guidance that such facilities should be provided in site toilets, but we should be asking why it is still not mandatory.[182] As I write this in 2024/2025, we continue to see women in the industry complaining about the lack of, or insufficient, welfare facilities available to them.

Summary

This chapter has homed in specifically on the issues women in UK construction face on a daily basis. Women are suffering from sexism and harassment and a staggering 62% of the women I surveyed said they had been bullied in the workplace.

Verbal and mental bullying and gaslighting is rife in the industry and the fact that 70% of the women who said they had reported bullying said they had been made to feel they were too emotional or sensitive reinforces the claim that women face a toxic culture.

We also have to acknowledge that women are not perfect either, in fact some women are just as toxic as some men can be and will go out of their way to bully and hurt other women. We need to educate and call out these behaviours just as much in women as we need to with men.

Women are suffering from a lack of parity in pay and often have additional difficulties with their career progression. They suffer further when they become mothers with many companies failing to properly support them. Women from minority groups, particularly related to race or ethnicity, suffer additional discrimination.

The industry needs to improve. If it is to become more inclusive, this means going back to basics. The industry needs to ensure people have PPE that fits and is made for their bodies; it needs to provide the necessary facilities on sites to ensure women and others with specific welfare needs are accounted for. We need to provide everyone with the facilities to enable them to thrive.

SIX
Role Models And Practical Advice For Women

When it comes to women as role models, I didn't really have many through much of my career as I was almost always the only woman in a sea of men.

I do believe that not having women as role models meant things were harder as I had no one to discuss the challenges with. While it may not have stopped me from pursuing my goals, I suspect if there had been more role models, particularly early in my career, it's possible that some of those other women on my university degree that left the industry may have stayed and perhaps even more would have joined.

Representation matters. One of the quotes I remember is, 'You can't be what you can't see', which came from Marian Wright Edelman, the founder and president of the Children's Defence Fund, in a 2011 documentary.[183] Perhaps the better known one is '… and if you can see it, you can be it', written by Billie Jean King in her autobiography *All In*.[184]

One woman who was a role model in my career was Maria Joyce at Wates Construction. A chartered surveyor and incredible cheerleader and support, Maria helped me get chartered and supported me through my Post Graduate Diploma in Law, and I was more than a little disappointed when our division was split in two and I was moved elsewhere in the business. Eventually I left and I often wonder would I have stayed had that split not happened? It's amazing how those we are surrounded by – both good and bad – can have such a deep impact on us and even make our career change direction.

This is why I know role models and mentors, supporters and sponsors are incredibly important, particularly when you are working in challenging and sometimes outright hostile environments in the construction industry.

Thankfully there are many more women role models in the industry now and I decided to speak to a few of them and get some practical advice that other women can use to help navigate through the issues we often face in construction and that these women themselves have had to work through. I also asked the women I surveyed to provide advice on how they would deal with some of the situations women face; while these are anonymised to protect confidentiality, they offer useful perspectives from others who have been through similar experiences. First let's take a look at representation of women generally.

Women who do make it in business

Traditionally, women have not been represented on boards, which were historically mostly comprised of men. This is changing and it is an important step in providing better representation for women, which in turn gives other women role models to see and aspire to.

Back in 2011, women only made up 9.5% of members on FTSE 350 company boards. Fast forward to February 2024 and the FTSE Leaders Review (an independent, business-led framework supported by the UK government) reported that over half of all FTSE 100 companies had met the 40% target of women in leadership ahead of the original December 2025 target.[185] It also found an all-time high had been reached of 42.1% for women on boards. The Leaders Review was developed to set recommendations for the UK's largest companies in order to improve the representation of women on boards and prior to this the numbers were measured by the Hampton-Alexander and Davies Review.

While this is positive, women need to be better represented in larger numbers for the four biggest roles of Chair, SiD, CEO and Finance Director and, sadly, seventy-seven FSTE 350 companies actually went backwards, with reductions of women in leadership positions.

When we look at construction specifically, it's evident from the research that no construction company appears in the top ten best performers overall. Of the top fifty private companies, Laing O'Rourke Corp Ltd features with 41% (down from 43% in 2023) of women being in leadership positions and Mace Group Ltd and Wates Group Ltd feature with 35% and 32% respectively. Laing features joint seventh for women on boards, with parity having been reached in 2023 as they hit 50%.

This shows us improvements can be, and are being, made, although it is sad to see that overall in the top fifty private companies the figure had dropped 0.8% between 2022 and 2023.

Forbes also reported that, as of March 2023, 10.4% of Fortune 500 companies were now led by women, with fifty-three women-led Fortune 500 companies compared to just four in the year 2000; this remained stable in 2024.[186]

In 2022, Costain added a fifth female director to its executive board.[187] Its Chief Financial Officer, Helen Willis, was named among the best paid in the construction industry for the first time, being the fifteenth best paid boss among building contractors listed in *Construction News* analysis, earning £802,055 (including a bonus of £394,200) in Costain's 2020 accounting year.[188] Costain is another construction company that has equal men and women on its board as of 2024.

However, generally construction is falling behind in respect of gender diversity, according to a Creditsafe report which found that, out of 458,761 firms operating in UK construction, only 21% have women represented at director level, the lowest across all sectors in the UK.[189]

In 2024, *Construction News* examined the top twenty largest firms and found board members to be mostly white and predominantly male.[190] It also found that while women on boards were better represented than women on site, most of the largest companies remain years behind other sectors.

So companies are improving.

Role models and allies in construction

A lot of work is needed to improve numbers of women in the industry, not just on boards but throughout. What are women in the industry doing to help?

The individuals listed here are women I have seen speak at conferences, followed on LinkedIn, worked with in my own career or been recommended to speak to by other women or men. I hope their wisdom helps anyone reading this book.

Please also remember these are not the only women doing great things, for example, in Chapter 3 I spoke about Katherine Evans and all her work around PPE. But this section gives some ideas and advice from women working hard to make things better, so seek them out, connect on LinkedIn and work together so everyone in construction can win.

Sandi Rhys Jones OBE talks about not apologising

Sandi, former President of the CIOB, said:

> 'Women don't have to do it all. The world is changed by people who turn up, and that does not mean having to do everything all the time. It is fine to say no. Learn to manage yourself in this regard; it takes practice but it's worth it.'

The other big thing we discussed was women's habit of saying 'sorry' all the time. Whether it's 'sorry I can't do that because' or 'sorry I'm just a project manager' or 'sorry I'm just an engineer', many women have a habit of apologising in advance even when they have nothing to apologise for. Sandi advises that 'Constantly saying sorry takes your power away. You do not need to apologise. Change the language! Saying sorry all the time simply stops you from being confident.'

The next time you're about to say sorry for something, take a step back and change the language. For example, suppose you are late to a meeting or late with a deadline, instead of saying 'sorry' why not flip it and simply say 'thank you for your patience' next time.

Changing our language can be incredibly empowering.

Ceri Evans talks boundaries

I saw Ceri speak a couple of years ago at a conference and I wanted to share her wisdom with you around the idea that, as women, we need to be strong enough to put in place our own boundaries.

Ceri explained that we all have things that are important to us outside of work; she calls these our 'red lines'. They can be related to children, spouse or partner, friends, or an art or exercise class you do regularly, for example.

Ceri says it's not just about saying this informally; it's important to negotiate your role so that your red lines are clear from the start. For example, one of my own 'red lines' is that every Friday I stop at 4pm as I have a personal training session. I make sure my work on that day starts early, or I work through lunch, and it's set in my calendar that I am out of the office and busy.

It's also important not to allow the 'red lines' to creep. If you allow it once you must make sure it's a one-off or else people will expect that you will bend your 'red lines' to suit them.

Ceri says it's also important as a leader to honour other people's red lines, for example don't set up meetings at the beginning or end of the day when parents may be dropping children to school or collecting them.

Boundaries create a sense of safety and if we actively set expectations and boundaries no one can ever be disappointed. It's not always easy though, especially when you're early in your career, and it's easy to get carried away and say 'yes' to everything we are asked or to worry if we say 'no' we may lose our job. With the benefit of hindsight from my thirty-year career in the construction industry, I can safely say I should have learned to say no a lot sooner than I did!

Jen Kelly encourages trades

I came across Jen's posts on LinkedIn and noticed she champions getting women into trades. Currently based in Australia, she set up Women In Trades Network Ireland in 2016 as she was struggling, even with experience, to get an apprenticeship on her home turf.[191] She is frank about the issues in the industry and, as with my research, has spoken to women who are still being asked if they want to have children or being told that employers only want men. She was recently included in 'The Image of Women in Construction' photographic project at National Association of Women In Construction (London & South East region), and photographer Morley von Sternberg FRIBA. Another great role model for other women who is currently undertaking a carpentry apprenticeship.

Deb Nutt talks being personal

I spoke to Deborah Nutt, a senior leader at Arcadis who I had the pleasure of spending some time with when I worked there. She's had a long career and we spoke about leadership in terms of teamwork and what she has learned to make herself a better leader.

Deb's advice was:

'Think of people and teams like the wheel of a bike. Everyone is a spoke in that wheel and we all play a part. If someone isn't performing, the wheel goes lumpy and as a leader you need to find out what's going on.'

Business is all about people and culture at the end of the day, we are all human and as a leader 'you need to show you are human and approachable, especially now we have more remote working, as young people in particular suffer due to less in-person contact'.

When something isn't right it's time to reach out. Deb says simple actions like drinking more coffee/tea can help: 'That fifteen- to twenty-minute chat can make a world of difference. Just really listening to someone and making time to find out what's going on with them can get them back to performing well very quickly.'

Sui Mun Li promotes networking

Sui Min Li is a highly experienced civil and structural engineer who won the National Federation of Builders (NFB) Top 100 most influential woman in construction as well as the award for local hero in 2023. When we spoke about her advice for other women, she said:

'There will be difficult times but try not to let it affect you. You can be whatever you want to be if you are passionate and have drive, but remember to network with others so that you have support and somewhere to go for advice.'

Recently Sui Min teamed up with Clare Friel, founder of Construction Anglia and MD of marketing agency Friel, to set up a women in construction networking event to provide inspiration to students.[192] This has been a great success, so much so that the students visited London Build 2024 to meet up with Sui Min and they have subsequently held a second larger event.

Sinead Molloy talks about welfare facilities

Sinead Molloy has had an extensive career spanning tunnelling, mining, rail, power, highways, commercial construction, and even property development. In 2021, she founded her business, She Built It, after leaving a previous role due to challenges she faced while working in a remote area. Like many women, Sinead's needs included access to clean facilities, especially during her menstrual cycle, but her workplace failed to provide adequate welfare provisions.

In one incident she had to drive to a nearby Tesco for necessities like using the bathroom or buying lunch. On this occasion, the Tesco restroom was out of order, so she was forced to drive forty-five minutes home to access clean facilities. Despite raising this issue and providing a solution to the reoccurring problem, it was criticised during her performance review, as though it was her problem to manage. This experience led Sinead to embarking on a mission to create her business, which supports, mentors, and connects women in trades with job opportunities. Today, she ensures that all companies and sites she works with provide the proper welfare facilities for their workers.

When I asked Sinead for advice for other women, she said, 'Remember, all eyes are on you. You might be the only woman, and people will always be watching, so work hard and know your craft.'

Sinead also offers clear advice to the industry:

> 'Do things differently for women. Provide the facilities they need. Offer a four-day workweek or flexible hours with later starts and earlier finishes. I've seen women accomplish just as much, if not more, under these options than with the traditional 7-to-5, five-day schedule. It's time to change the way we work.'

Anonymous encourages people-first management

One woman who preferred not to be named has come through difficult experiences with an appreciation that it's all about people:

> 'I have been bullied in many workplaces by men and women. Architecture and construction can be very toxic environments. These experiences

have given me strength to focus on a people-first approach in terms of management – I will never let anyone else feel like this.'

Michaela Wain talks goal setting

Previously on BBC's *The Apprentice,* Michaela is a force to be reckoned with and she has a passion for helping women in construction. A business owner of a construction magazine, she works hard to promote women. She set up a networking group for women and she also offers training and helps women access grants to undertake it. She also set up the Design and Build Women in Construction Award (in their fourth year in 2024) to publicise women and celebrate their achievements.

While Michaela doesn't have direct experience of working on site like many of the women I have spoken to or surveyed, she listens to the issues women are facing and wants to help find solutions.

When I asked Michaela what her advice would be for women in the industry, she had a few ideas. Being part of a network and having male allies came top. As a business owner, Michaela has had struggles, but she attributes her success to the fact she steps into her fear and is strict about goal setting. She does this each year, setting out business, personal and pleasure goals and she keeps track of them every quarter. Her final bit of advice to women who may be struggling was, 'Don't hold yourself back. Life is a gamble. If you aren't happy right now, ask why and then make the decision to change it. Leave if you need to.'

Carol Massay says stop and think

When Dr Massay started in the industry, there was no support, there were few (if any) female role models and there was no social media. When difficulties occurred, she had to navigate her own way through situations. We discussed some of the harassment she had experienced in her career, and the thing that came out of our discussion was to stop and think:

> 'Think through the situation and ask yourself, "Do I react, and if I do, will it bring more attention, or do I choose another route?" There are times when it's best to ignore things and think, "I am not going to let someone in power put me in a position where I have to leave because of them," but there may also be times where the situation is one that cannot be laughed off or ignored and you may need to report or leave for your own mental health. Use your support network to discuss the issues and help you to decide on the best approach for the situation at hand.'

Role models and advice from outside of the industry

It's not just women in construction who can have challenging times at work. In this section I set out advice drawn from women who have faced similar experiences in other settings.

Mandy Hickson talks about speaking up

Mandy Hickson's *An Officer Not a Gentlemen* describes the challenges she faced in joining the RAF and becoming the second woman to fly the Tornado fighter jet. Her story has some brilliant examples of male allyship from her course mates (something I discuss in Chapter 8) but her experience overlaps in many ways with the difficulties faced by women in construction.

I spoke to Mandy after an introduction from former RAF fighter pilot Dheeraj Bhasin MBE, who I interview later in the book. I asked her how she dealt with some of the issues related to gender in the RAF and what advice she would perhaps give herself or indeed other women now.

She noted that, as with construction in days gone by, the RAF had a pretty strong drinking culture. Mandy, like myself, had often endeavoured to 'fit in' by using humour, a potty mouth, acting less feminine and just trying to knuckle down and prove herself.

She also said that one of the things that was a real issue for her (aside from some of the behaviours) was the PPE. Mandy had to wear PPE made for men, something scarily familiar to most women in construction. She similarly had issues where there was no women's toilet. At the time, because the career was her passion, she just put up with these things and let them go.

In retrospect, she says:

'It's not OK to have to fit in like I did. We are all chameleons to some extent but we don't need to do this and my advice to women would be don't let things go when they aren't right. Call it out. Don't compromise you.'

When it came to talking about the bullying Mandy encountered when on tour in the Gulf, it was clear it had (as with anyone being bullied) been a difficult time and it had taken its toll. She became withdrawn and isolated and it was only her husband's support and her tenacity that meant she stayed.

On bullying, Mandy said:

'Again, call it out. But find a wingman, someone to support you and if you can, have them there with you when you try to talk to the person concerned. Ensure there is no emotion, stick to the facts and evidence. Write it down if you need to and say things like, "When you say X it makes me feel like Y." But do call it out.'

That said, we agreed that sadly some people who bully will not change even when you bring it to their attention.

If you are experiencing bullying, it is important to safeguard yourself and consider your options. This may mean reporting the situation to management and/or HR and considering leaving a company if the situation is not properly addressed. The most important thing is to look after yourself and your mental health.

Helen Chorley says be yourself

Previously an investment banker who worked on the trading floor, Helen now works as a property investor. Her advice for women, based on her experience in the equally macho and male trading-floor arena, is that women do not have to be like, dress like or act like men. She said:

> 'One of the biggest things women need to learn is to have boundaries. As women we need to think about how we want to be treated at work. Ask yourself, how do I want to be spoken to?
>
> 'If something happens that is outside of your boundaries, think about how you will express yourself. It's OK to say no and it's OK to be you. Life is too short to pretend and doing that will simply make you tired and burnt out.'

Eugenie Brooks says stay strong when being bullied

I met Eugenie because she used to be my partner's Sergeant when they were both working in the Metropolitan Police.

Eugenie was a trailblazer in the police, serving for thirty-three years in various departments from foot duty, traffic and Royalty Protection to firearms supervisor by the time she retired. She was also the first ever woman supervisor on the SEG (Special Escort Group on motorbikes). It wasn't always easy, unsurprisingly, and she was harassed and bullied at times. She tried various things like we all do, putting up with it because it was easier, standing up for herself (which got her labelled as a troublemaker or isolated) and at one point she was given, in her words, 'shit postings' and having her life made a misery because she'd complained.

She admitted that even she as a woman had bias and thought women who complained were a problem but eventually she realised she had to formally complain to her Federal Rep about how she was being treated. Sadly, while she had support from one colleague most others ignored her, which was hard. Eventually she asked to be moved.

Eugenie admits:

> '[The sexist treatment] made me cry… but it's not a sign of weakness, for me it was pure frustration and anger at the way I was being treated. It did in fact help me – I got rid of my anger through the tears, dried my eyes, looked in the locker room mirror and was determined not to let them grind me down. It made me stronger. I used to say to myself – I'm the daughter of a decorated fighter pilot and will not let these sexist idiots grind me down.'

Her advice for when women are dealing with bullying and harassment was clear:

> 'Stay strong and talk to someone, create your network and lean on them. Remember you are not there to be a punch bag, you're there to do a job. Don't be frightened to go to a union, HR or ask to be moved or leave if you need to. Your mental health and happiness is worth way more than any job.'

Carolyn Hobdey talks self-investment

I was introduced to Carolyn thanks to mutual connections I met at the Top 100 awards in 2023. Carolyn has written three books and one of the things I liked about her when we spoke is that she feels the same as me in that, while things are bad and need to change, demonising men is not the way to go about it.

We need to communicate and make it safe for men to talk and learn and we as women also need to learn. When I asked what her advice to women would be, she said:

> 'Women don't invest time and money into themselves. We must prioritise ourselves because we are worth investing in. Experiences may have hurt us but if you suppress it you won't heal. Do the work on yourself, ask what is the wound, what triggers it and what needs to heal and then invest in what you need whether that's with time, money, doing a course or having therapy.'

Toni Hargis provides comebacks

I spoke to Toni Hargis after reading *How to Stand up to Sexism*, a book she wrote with BritMums that is designed to provide women with 'comebacks' to use in situations where they are dealing with sexism, microaggressions, insults or worse.[193] When I first read it I had mixed feelings – a combination of, 'I wish I had known to say that,' mixed with, 'Wow, in my industry if I said that response it could inflame the situation and make it worse.' When we spoke about this Toni was clear that it's down to us as individuals to choose the relevant response to use. There is no right or wrong when standing up to sexism but stand up to it we must. Therefore I would ask all women *and* men reading this book to also read Toni's and consider how they can do things differently next time they are faced with sexism or microaggressions.

Advice from the women surveyed for the book

The women who completed my survey were given the opportunity to provide advice to other women to help them navigate through some of the issues they may face working in the industry. These comments are anonymised to protect the women who took part, but I have shared some of their advice below.

What advice would you give to a woman who is being bullied by a colleague?

'SPEAK OUT! Report it immediately. Be brave and know that the world can only change if we are brave enough to change it. Find a female or a male ally in the business as a sounding board if you don't have the strength to go to HR straight away, don't ignore it. It will not stop, unless you do something.'

'1) Document every occasion, no matter how minor. When it was, what was done and said and how it made you feel in that moment. This creates an undeniable base if the issue needs to be discussed or escalated. 2) Do tell someone you trust about it to share the challenge and for that individual to potentially be a support when you do formally report it. 3) Find out your company's process and follow it. You can ask for a private discussion in the first instance, and you can always ask to have someone with you to support you. But please report it – you never know who else is being impacted by this individual and you may help them while helping yourself.'

'I'm not a confrontational person and the situation I was in, everyone knew about it but couldn't do anything about it. They weren't going to fire him or even discipline him. They let him get away with it. Eventually I had to leave for my own mental health. But I will say this, getting the phone call to say they wanted me barely an hour after the interview was a huge confidence boost. And to move somewhere that actually appreciates you is so much better. So, even though it may be scary, removing yourself from the situation is sometimes the best course of action.'

'Report and if no action, find another job.'

'Call it out, regardless of whether you have support or not. Do not suffer in silence. If you call it out and nothing is done about it, you will realise this is not the place for you. And you never know just by vocalising your concerns, you may trigger growth/change in someone or in the company, this may not happen immediately but it may happen with time. Also you may give other females or minorities within the company a voice.'

'Document it and report it; do not let it go unnoticed. Do not bear this burden alone. This will ebb away at you and start to destroy your self-confidence, self-worth and even cause you to doubt your career in construction. No matter how petty or small you may think it is, report and get support.'

'Keep a diary – date, time, what happened and how it made you feel. Once you've got a log – just a simple Excel spreadsheet saved on your desktop – you can review it and decide what is the best way to tackle it:

speak to someone senior, approach HR, speak to them directly, raise a formal grievance, etc.'

What advice would you give to a woman receiving inappropriate sexual advances?

'Exactly the same as bullying. I know this situation too many times when I was younger and my only regret is to not have done something at the time because I know those men that initiate this kind of verbal or physical abuse don't stop with one female. They continue to find victims. They must be stopped; the behaviour has to be reported and stopped. Be brave.'

'Call it out if you can, if you feel uncomfortable find an ally, get support and don't be afraid of ramifications. They're in the wrong.'

'We must be very clear to the "perpetrator", even if it means hurting their feelings/ego. If we get called a "bitch" for turning down/standing up for ourselves the problem lies with them, not us. This is perhaps where a male ally would be useful.'

'Get yourself safe. Report it. If nothing happens report it again. Avoid situations which might endanger you.'

'To speak up to a manager or HR. Even if it is hard or uncomfortable. Keep a log of what, when and where this behaviour occurred.'

'Be honest, tell him clearly and calmly that you're not interested. If he doesn't stop, speak to your immediate manager ASAP. If someone doesn't take no for an answer, they may be dangerous. Don't ever find yourself on your own with him.'

'Depends on the situation, go to a trusted colleague, report it if it's persistent, be very clear with the person it is unwanted.'

What advice would you give a woman who is coming back from maternity leave?

'Explain if you are feeling nervous having been away but express enthusiasm about coming back. Work out a part-time to full-time route (if appropriate) using leave to ease yourself into the new routine. Take up any offers of returner training. Read around your subject and know what is going on in your field generally.'

'Ensure there is an initial return to work meeting where you're updated with key information/news that you were absent for. Have a few keeping in touch style meetings before your return if you can, or an informal visit or two to your workplace before the first shift back. Be open to a different workplace than the one you left, and don't accept any kind of negativity or inappropriate comments or behaviour around your situation.'

'Don't expect work to be easy after having kids as there is added pressure when time off is needed etc. It's a juggling act but not one that lasts forever!'

'You have literally just grown, birthed and started raising a child. You are a superwoman who has just gone through one of the biggest learning curves that life can offer. So come back to work with that attitude. You do not have to prove yourself to anyone. Just continue to do your job to the best of your ability as you were before the baby came along.'

'I have just returned to work after a near-double maternity leave and I would suggest:

1. If possible, ensure you are ready to return – I returned when my second child was nine months and now feel I was not ready and should have waited until she was twelve months but financially I felt forced to return.
2. Use Keeping-in-Touch days if available.
3. Phase yourself back into work slowly.
4. Keep in contact with colleagues throughout to keep in the loop.
5. Be gentle on yourself. It is like starting a new job and I have felt very overwhelmed – learning new colleagues' names, roles/new processes/changes to business/changes in industry. You cannot be expected to deliver 100% from day 1.
6. Being organised is the only way I have (vaguely) coped with transition back to full-time working in

> a busy construction company with two under two at home.'

What do women want from industry?

One of the things that needs to improve for women is the support they receive. In my survey it is clear women do not think DEI is doing what it should, with only 20% of women surveyed saying they thought enough was being done to address the key issues and empower women. A staggering 245 of the 302 women surveyed (81%) said they think companies simply say they are doing things to create equal opportunities to 'look good' to the public.

When I asked women if they thought DEI policies actually work, 51 said yes, 59 said no and 192 said most of the time. What was more concerning was that 39% of the women surveyed said that men challenge DEI targets and policies as being 'unfair' or 'stacked against men'.

Women do not want to be treated differently because they are women, they want to have the same opportunities to succeed; however, 41% of the women I surveyed (125 of the 302) felt DEI initiatives can send out the signal (wrongly) that women need more 'help' to succeed or aren't as capable.

The most concerning response was to the question *'Do you think D, E & I policies mean women are taken less seriously as men think they only got the job to tick the diversity box?'* Sadly, 63% of the women I surveyed think they are taken less seriously by men.

So how do we tackle these issues? The women I surveyed also had some good insights into this as well:

'Actions speak louder than words on a policy document. Visible actions need to be taken in line with DEI targets. Also better, clearer, more in-depth explanations to other staff as to why these are in place, why they're needed, and the benefits to all of a diverse and inclusive workplace.'

'Targets are so easy to write. The organisational behaviours repeated daily to achieve those targets are really, really hard; improvements need to be made in:

- Visibility and availability of role models
- Collation of Intel of why staff are leaving
- Robust investment in activity to respond to the issues identified in exit interviews
- Ongoing consultation with staff to find out if activities are working
- Creating or investing more in mentoring/business buddy schemes to create allies across the business
- More stories "from the individual" people using their own words and phrases – not polished media case studies, to help inspire, encourage and motivate existing staff.'

'At the moment it's done as a tick-box exercise. Every session on promoting these kinds of measures is "optional" and it's ALWAYS attended by the same people, who aren't really the ones who need it!'

'Training on why DEI is important and to help people see their own privilege.'

'Provide external mentors. Review the business's existing policies and make required changes to make it a sustainable place to work for females.'

'Mandatory CPD [continuing professional development] on the subject is a good start.'

'Awareness and training for ALL employees, male and female.'

Summary

It is evident we have numerous interlinking issues in the industry and that things need to change. However, there are women who thrive and succeed but even those who succeed can find the pressure takes its toll.

There are some amazing advocates and role models in and outside the industry who have provided some great advice for women to use. However, unless we change the system and culture we are all working in, we will still find we continue to bring women into the industry and later lose them due to our leaky pipeline.

The only way to retain the talent we have and to improve diversity moving forward is for us to accept the issues that are prevalent in the industry. We cannot deny there are serious issues of sexism, bullying and gender bias and we need to work to create policies that tackle these issues.

Most of all, women want the industry to stop paying lip service to DEI and for companies to provide better and perhaps mandatory training as it is clear that some issues could be solved with proper education. It needs to be done in the right way, using real experiences to enable those who perhaps do not understand the issues women face to realise the issues that are there.

PART THREE
MALE ROLE MODELS, ALLIES, INSTITUTIONAL CHANGE AND MENTORS TO WOMEN

SEVEN
How Can Men Help?

Women can speak about the issues we face and tell our stories and ask for men to be allies, but part of that involves asking men to understand the differences between how we are treated on a daily basis (not excepting other groups who often have things even tougher).

The fact is white men in particular have an advantage over women. This is not any man's fault who may be reading this book today; it is the result of years of the patriarchy built long ago. It is a result of history, of unconscious bias of our learnings and surroundings and the way we are raised.

Often we do not understand why things are the way they are but if we refuse to look at another perspective things will never change. It's like that old saying about not judging someone until you have put yourself in their shoes – we must do this to understand the issues at play and it goes both ways.

Once we understand the issues faced by women and men (yes, that's right, I include men here) as a result of years of patriarchy, then we can work on ways to prevent history from repeating and improving things for everyone.

So first let's take a quick look at the patriarchy and how, as a result of that, we are left with a world in which *we are all suffering* and then look at allyship and how that can help make things better for women and men (and other marginalised and minority groups).

The patriarchy – what is it?

The word patriarchy emanates from the Greek word *patriaekhe* and in its literal sense it means 'the rule of the father'. It is used to refer to a system where the social beliefs, systems and/or values that are embedded in social, political and economic systems disproportionately put men in control, creating inequality between men and women. This can vary between cultures, but the main characteristic is that men will hold more power and authority.

Historically, it may have been where the father/male leader/elder/religious leader had total authority over the family or community as a whole.

For those of you who may have seen the 2023 Greta Gerwig Barbie film (or been cajoled to go by your partner perhaps) the patriarchy was shown brilliantly, everything was flipped. Barbies were in charge of everything (matriarchy) and were able to succeed unencumbered. They had masculine traits; they created and maintained Barbieland independently, whereas Kens were shown to be emasculated, insecure, often grovelling men without purpose who 'needed' Barbie(s).

While there is much more to the film, it was a brilliantly clever way of showing patriarchy in action (even if I didn't personally like the ending) and it sparked a lot of debate on social media; it even led to Sir Robert McAlpine doing a Barbie-in-construction post on LinkedIn, which *CIOB People* then wrote about because of some of the comments the post attracted.[194]

Why do I mention it? Because if anyone does not understand how patriarchy affects women in Western society, the film is a brilliant way of showing it. However, patriarchy is also damaging to men.

Let me explain. First, ignore the fact that generally in many cultures the patriarchy has traditionally meant that men have privileges and power over women, thus creating gender inequality. Let's take a look at what it means for children, for our boys and girls as they grow up.

Boys have historically been taught and brought up, for example, here in the West in a certain way. We see this in the games they play, the groups they join and the expectations that are held of them by society.

Here are just a few elements of the patriarchy that are taught to young boys and men that are damaging to men:

- Boys are often taught to dominate and to be in control from a young age. While this may provide a sense of power it also means men have unfair expectations on them to be strong and in control all the time as they grow into adulthood.

- Boys are often pushed to be loud and aggressive and applauded for such things in some sports whereas the opposite is true for girls.

- Boys are generally not offered the opportunity to try what may be considered more traditionally 'female' sports and activities (eg ballet, hockey or netball); they are often pushed into more 'male' sports like rugby and football from a young age, despite these other options being equally good team sports and forms of exercise.

- Boys and men are often told not to share their emotions – 'Real Men don't cry', men must be self-reliant, 'suck it up', 'man up' etc. Men suffer mentally because they may feel shame about feeling vulnerable and expressing emotions like fear or worry.

- Men are often in constant competition with other men, trying to be stronger, earn more, have a better home, family, better holidays etc. This competition is ingrained to the extent that some men will work all hours to provide these material expectations but then hardly know their family, spend time at home or be able to enjoy the fruits of their labour.

- Men are often still expected to be the 'breadwinner' or 'main earner' in society and when they aren't they can feel undervalued because this is considered 'against the norm'.

- Men are often seen as the 'babysitter' or just 'helping mummy out' when they help with childcare and if they are a 'stay at home dad' many men (and sadly some women) will make fun of them. The fact is that for years men have lost huge opportunities to bond and create relationships with their children because patriarchy says mum should do the childcare and dad should go to work. Is that fair on mum, dad and the children?

- The patriarchy excludes LGBTQIA+ men.

If we then conversely look at what the patriarchy has done, and in many cases still does, to girls as they grow up and become women, we see things are equally difficult as while women now have rights to vote, work and have our own bank accounts, for example, the patriarchal expectations are still damaging to young girls and women.

- **Physical differences:** From a young age, girls are often taught they must hide their bodies, so while their little boy counterparts run around the park with their tops off girls are taught (despite the fact they look the same at young ages) they must keep their top on. In puberty girls then start to feel anxiety and shame as a result of their physical changes.

- **Play:** Girls at a young age are often handed dolls or the cooking set etc as a rehearsal for the patriarchal role of reproducer and caregiver, whereas boys will often be given trucks and space ships and rarely toys that relate to chores at home.

- **Sports:** Girls are often pushed to more 'female' sports such as ballet, netball or gymnastics rather than being given opportunities to try more traditionally male sports like football or rugby.

- **Assertiveness:** Girls are told they are bossy in situations where boys will be told they are assertive. This even plays out in schools and nurseries, as Dr Sabrina Cohen-Hatton wrote in her book *The Gender Bias*,[195] where she describes hearing her daughter's nursery teacher chastise her daughter for being 'bossy' while playing and tell her no one would want to play with her if she was 'bossy'.

- **Behaviour:** Girls and boys are often treated differently at a young age, even at school, with subtle messages communicating to them that there are certain ways to behave – such as 'be a good girl', reinforcing that girls are expected to be well behaved and compliant, compared to 'boys will be boys', which reinforces toughness and physicality and assumes tolerance for aggression or misbehaviour.

- **Careers:** As noted in Chapter 1, formulation of gender bias happens in children, and by the age of six it is fully formed in their subconscious. If boys are told they can be race car drivers and fighter pilots and girls are told they can be nurses or teachers is it any wonder so many girls think they will be no good at STEM subjects?

- **Appearance:** As girls grow into women they are consistently bombarded with depictions of the woman's body being sexualised and scrutinised, with adverts for makeup, anti-aging potions, hair dyes etc telling us that women's bodies are sexual and that women aren't good enough the way they are. As women age, the pressure seems to increase, with the idea that women should stay as young-looking as possible.

Thankfully awareness means that some of the above in respect of boys and girls is changing. I know my niece, for example, loves pink and purple and unicorns (totally her choice) but also likes dinosaurs and construction sets. She even played football for some time and much of this has been because she has been offered all these opportunities and not been influenced because of her gender.

However, even with parents trying their best to educate children to show them they can do any role, at some point the patriarchy will come into play as Ceri Evans found recently with her daughter. Ceri posted the experience on LinkedIn as her daughter at five years old (and despite having a mum who is passionate about construction showcasing it to her) suddenly told her 'I don't want this one anymore – it's a boy costume' in respect of her builder costume.

So why do I say the patriarchy harms men and women?

The patriarchy thrives on the premise that women are weak and men are tough, and this actually disempowers women and puts a lot of pressure on men. It is constant pressure and it can be damaging to men's mental and physical health.

The patriarchy puts expectations on men and women, and we need to work together to change these things for everyone, especially in construction.

Male privilege – do men really have it?

We have looked at the patriarchy and why it's so damaging to men and women but now let's look at the difference in the way men and women are treated and how this directly affects both genders throughout our lives and careers.

Some people refer to this as 'privilege' and I have to say I hate the word! I know it's a word that turns many people off but while I have the statistics from my research showing there are real differences between the way women and men are treated (and there is a barrage of other research out there that says the same), often using this word can cause considerable friction when we try to discuss it with friends, colleagues and peers.

In trying to unpack this I decided to first look at what the word privilege actually means. The Cambridge Dictionary defines privilege as 'an advantage that only one person or group of people has, usually because of their position or because they are rich'.[196]

It seems simple, doesn't it? I can't go into a full history lesson on where the phrase came from, but one well-recognised description appears in Peggy McIntosh's groundbreaking essay in 1988, 'White Privilege: Unpacking the Invisible Knapsack', in which she helped readers recognise what white privilege was, by making its effects easy to see using various examples such as:

- Being able to walk into a shop and find tights in your skin tone
- Turning on the television and seeing people of your race widely represented
- Being able to walk down the street without being racially profiled or unfairly stereotyped.

Whether we like the word or not, the simple fact is that it's invisible to many, it's often there and it's often linked to gender, race, sexual orientation, religion, ability or social standing (or some other difference).

It's clear many people find the word difficult to deal with and it can make people feel defensive, something I discussed with certified neurosculpting facilitator and coach Jo Britton.[197] She explained strong reactions can be a result of our conditioning and because our brain feels our status is somehow being attacked or threatened.

For this book I decided to look not only at the phrase itself but also at the actual issues instead and identify what advantages and disadvantages some people may or may not have been born with and/or have over each other instead.

It's important to point out that just because a man may benefit from male privilege this doesn't mean his life is easy or that he has not had struggles. It simply means the struggles and hurdles are not because of his gender.

I know for some men I have spoken to during the course of writing this book, even the suggestion that women may have disadvantages compared to them merely because of their gender can cause immediate defensiveness and sometimes outright anger and denial.

One example is a white man who had a difficult childhood and didn't have much money and had to work really hard to get where he is. How can that put him at an advantage versus, say, a white middle-class woman whose family put her through private school or university?

Now while it's true that not all men will have access to the same privileges as others because of race, ethnicity, nationality, class, education, employment status, sexual orientation and appearance, if we look at an average white heterosexual male in the West, he will generally, as a result of the patriarchy we have already discussed, have advantages over a white woman before either of them even utters a word.

If we look further into advantages related to race, a white woman like me will often have an advantage over a black woman or an Asian woman.

Mary Ann Sieghart wrote about some of these issues in her book *The Authority Gap*,[198] where she catalogues various everyday biases in society that create the gap that persists between men and women, leading to men often being taken more seriously than women and women being judged unfairly. She discusses various stereotypes and biases and how these hinder women and have traditionally been used to keep women in their place and offer advantages to men.

One thing I am pretty sure most people can agree on is that this isn't right or fair, but we cannot deny it is there.

To make it easier for us to understand how these unseen advantages may affect us personally, here's a really simple exercise that was provided to me by Kat Parsons. It aims to enable us to understand the advantages or disadvantages we may have over others without even realising it.[199]

Put-a-finger-down exercise

Hold up all fingers on both hands and read the following statements, putting down a finger each time it applies to you. Put a finger down...

1. If you've ever hesitated to disclose your partner's gender identity to a work colleague

2. If you ever struggled to find 'nude' plasters or products (foundation/tights) in your skin tone

3. If you need digital docs to be in a certain format (eg PDF) that is legible for your screen reader

4. If you would think twice about calling the police if a situation required their help

5. If you have ever had someone refer to you using the wrong pronouns

6. If you struggle to work in loud, crowded, colourful spaces as it's a sensory overwhelm

7. If your family would be unable to offer you financial support if you needed it

8. If you don't feel safe going for a jog at night or in a poorly lit, empty neighbourhood

9. If you have to scrutinise holiday destinations to make sure you'll be safe to vacation there

10. If you've ever been to an interview where none of the recruitment panel looks like you

You can see how a white heterosexual man would be left with more fingers held up than would a white woman, a white gay man, a black man or a man who is neuro-diverse, for example, or indeed how a white cis woman would have more fingers up compared to a black woman or a white trans woman. I actually did this exercise at the *Construction News* and *New Civil Engineer* Inspiring Women in Construction Conference

2023. I had a fabulously diverse panel with me, and I got all 300 people in the room up on their feet (if they were able) and with both hands up in the air. The room was quiet as I read through those statements and then silent as I asked people to look around and see the advantages they had (that they may not have even been aware of) compared to others in the room.

If you want to try another more interactive exercise, go onto the BBC website and take part in their race *The Ally Track*,[200] which shows visually what advantages you may have over others, or go onto the Better Allies[201] website and look at the various lists of '50 Potential Privileges in the Workplace' sheets and think about how not having these may impact someone else's experience.

One thing I want everyone reading this to know is that *it's OK for us to not have fully appreciated the unwritten advantages and disadvantages that may be present*. What is important in the first instance is that we acknowledge them, instead of trying to deny them or make excuses as to why we do not believe it to be true (yes, I have had a number of debates with people over this in the past few years as to why they do not think they have any privilege or advantage over others).

Another thing I have had to accept in researching and writing this book is we can't change everyone. Some people are so deeply entrenched in their own denial that they refuse to believe they have any advantages over others and it's simply a waste of time and energy to try and educate them otherwise. Discuss it with someone once or twice by all means, but if they still refuse to see any other view give up and move on. Life is too short to be wasting energy on people who do not want to learn or grow.

Part of what led to me writing this book was learning that women from other minorities that weren't white, like me, had suffered even worse struggles than I and other white women had. For me, my sense of fairness and justice sees this as completely unacceptable and that's why I want change to happen, and I hope that's why you are reading this book – so you can join me in making the change.

I spoke to two people who have recently had the realisation of just how differently men and women are treated and how these advantages can play out in two very different ways.

I discovered the first one almost by accident. During the process of writing the book, an article popped up in my LinkedIn feed from Moxy – The Voice of Women in Infrastructure, about a man called Dan who had an epiphany about gender equality after attending a session entitled 'Maintaining a Competitive Advantage with Your Greatest Resource – Women' at a conference where Moxy founder Natasha Ozybko was speaking.[202]

Dan admitted he attended feeling pretty defensive but came away with a new realisation that even he was inadvertently contributing to gender inequality both at work and at home.

I contacted Dan and asked if we could speak because it is this kind of realisation that I suspect many men could have (and indeed I and most women and marginalised groups want them to have) and I wanted to know more.

Luckily for me Dan said yes and we had a great conversation, but when we spoke Dan admitted he hadn't even told his wife and family about the article and my first reaction was to immediately tell him when he went home he absolutely had to tell them as they would think he was amazing.

Dan was worried about reactions to his article and this was understandable. Part of being a male ally is speaking up and, while he'd done that to the magazine, Dan had been concerned about putting his head above the parapet elsewhere in other parts of his life. It was great to hear that of course all his family and friends thought it was amazing and even better to see a couple of weeks later that he posted about it himself on LinkedIn.

When we spoke, aside from now having the understanding of the little things that can make a difference to equality (women clearing up after an office lunch or being expected to be the note taker in a meeting for example), it was great to see that Dan had created a ripple effect with the article at work. He had been having discussions with other men who had read it and in doing so was creating awareness in others so that they too would start to learn about the issues.

As Dan said, 'We are all a product of our upbringing, the things we have read, the schools we attended, the TV we watched, the experiences we had, it's in your DNA. It doesn't mean you're a bad guy, it just means you weren't aware. So becoming aware of those biases and then changing your actions is what makes the difference.'

Then I found a second source that was able to explain exactly how white male privilege works from his own direct experience. George Evans transitioned from a white woman to a white man and he agreed to speak to me as he too was shocked at the difference in the way he was treated post transition.

George said his first real realisation of how men are treated differently was a softer experience and it involved getting the bus at university. As a white woman he had often forgotten the correct change but the bus driver more often than not would greet 'her' with 'don't worry love just get on' or 'you can pay with that beautiful smile' and such like. All little comments that many women hear on a daily basis and just ignore and move on. However, post transition, when he got on the bus as a white man without the correct change, the response from the same bus driver was starkly different – it was a clear, 'Sorry mate, you can't get on then.'

Then George was introduced to the alternate and more common moment where he understood exactly how differently white men are often treated compared to white women. George and his partner went for their mortgage meeting. He said:

> 'The entire time the advisor was just looking at me and talking to me, asking me the questions. Even when I didn't know the answer and referred to my partner he still directed everything

at me. It was like she was hardly there even though she knew the answers and I didn't.'

So privilege can work both ways, good and bad. Yes, a woman may get to ride the bus if she doesn't have sufficient money (and this definitely may be considered an advantage to some) but equally she will be downplayed and overlooked in other scenarios and these are the ones that, more often than not, affect things like career progression, promotion and pay rises for women.

We cannot ignore these experiences and George openly talks about this for the very reason that he now sees the real differences between the way white men and women are treated.

Male allies – why be one?

This book is specifically looking at the gender issues for women in construction. It's looking at the issues women face on a daily basis and how we can improve things for the industry as a whole.

This does not mean there are no other issues that need to be dealt with and my values are that we should all be able to come to work and be treated with fairness and respect whomever we are or however we identify. However, for this book I can only comment on my experiences as a woman in my thirty years in the construction industry and my research has been with hundreds of other women and men who also work in this industry.

So the next question I have for you is this: Now you have a realisation about the advantages you may have over others what can you actually do about it?

In the context of women in construction, this is literally a call out to the men working in the industry to join me and make the change.

First, here's what we don't need:

- Women don't need a man to come in and save the day.

- Women don't need hundreds of women's networks (although we acknowledge there are benefits to these).

- Women don't need lots of leadership courses (although we do know they have a place).

- Women don't need confidence coaching or lessons in how to ignore imposter syndrome (although these can be useful).

Why do we not *need* the above? Quite simply because women don't need fixing! All of the above assume women are incapable or the issues can be resolved by women simply working on themselves.

I highly recommend a book by Laura Bates, *Fix the System, Not the Women*, in which she systematically breaks down the many ways women are blamed for problems that in fact arise as a direct result of society not having been built by or indeed for women.[203]

Fixing women is not the solution.

Women did not create the system we live in. While I am a firm believer in the fact that we should always be learning and working on ourselves, doing that work does not solve the systemic issues and barriers women and other minority groups have to deal with, either in construction or globally.

What women do need is help to change the system and the biases that are currently at play so that they can succeed. To be precise, while any allies are good, we need male allies who can help challenge poor behaviours and biases around us and in other men in the industry. Why do we need men? As Mary Ann Sieghart's research for her book showed, the authority gap is real and it damages women's standing in the world.

We therefore need men who can work with men and women to challenge this gap and change the culture and environments we work in for the better, so that women in the future can avoid the struggles I and so many other women have had (and continue to have now).

But women also understand being a male ally to women may not be an easy path. In my research 67% of the women I surveyed understood that while equality needs men as allies, it's not always an easy path for men to take (especially if you don't know you may inadvertently be part of the problem). We get it!

The construction industry can be toxic in certain areas and women know men have their own struggles as well, particularly when standing up for women and working to make change happen.

Having gender equality does not mean men will be worse off or are being positively discriminated against, but we also cannot escape the fact that there is currently a big backlash against gender equality with many thinking that women's rights have gone too far.

In 2020, US research by the Pew Research Center found that 22% of Americans said that women's gains towards gender equality had come at the expense of men.[204] This view was more common among men (28%) than women (17%).

Research by Ipsos UK and the Global Institute for Women's Leadership at King's College London in 2023 studied thirty-two countries and found there was a growing sense of fear in respect of gender equality.[205] In fact, 29% of the British public said they were scared to speak out and advocate for equal rights of women because of what might happen to them.

Sadly the 2024 study is even more concerning, reporting that 47% of Britons say that when it comes to giving women equal rights with men, things have gone far enough in Great Britain (up from 38% in 2023), yet 43% of the UK population disagree that women's equality has gone far enough.[206] This shows how difficult the topic is and may go some way to explaining why there is often pushback when trying to get men to become allies to women in the fight for equality.

So why should you become an ally (especially in the face of this backlash)?

I've spoken to many men over the past few years researching my book and they have various 'whys' which I hope will help men reading this. One of my favourites came from Warren Stapley.

I saw Warren speak at a conference the RICS ran in March 2023 for International Women's Day. He's a former corporate finance lawyer turned DEI and Responsible Business Specialist who openly discusses his disability, a severe hearing impairment since birth. He is also a queer rights advocate, being part of the LGBTQIA+ community himself.

Anti-racism and intersectionality are particular focal points of Warren's inclusion work, but post the RICS conference (and a fair few messages between us), it struck me how much frustration he and others also feel in respect of the journey towards achieving gender parity. As Warren said at the conference, 'there is no need to fix women. Women are fine. We need to fix the system'.

Such words are perhaps unsurprising considering Warren had a strong female influence in his upbringing, with many independent women as role models, and he:

'... grew up watching women be strong, solve problems, deal with life and not be dependent on men for their identities and so, as an adult, I baulk at what constitutes "leadership" in so many professional service firms. So for me not being an "ally" would be a genuine betrayal of my entire upbringing.'

Warren said the same as me in that he also wants to see more men at these 'women's events' but 'also in workplaces and publicly calling out the misogyny and sexism that plagues this industry and others'. The way to make change happen is to stop concentrating only on women; as Warren says:

> 'Expecting women, as the oppressed here, to "solve" their own oppression while ignoring the role of men is like asking Black people and those of the Global Majority to bear all the effort of anti-racism work while ignoring the role of white people.'

Warren clearly has a passion to naturally ally himself to women and this is in part because of his lived experience and upbringing.

So for his advice to other men, I asked Warren the question I have asked all the men who have helped with my research. Why should other men ally themselves to women? Warren's response was that:

> '... in any equality campaign, in any facet of inclusion, it is only fair that the dominant majority take responsibility for driving change. For matters of gender equality within our patriarchal societies, this dominant majority is made up of men, whose power is related to their privilege. This is not a "woman's issue" to be fought for by wives, daughters, sisters and indeed merely by anyone identifying as female. It is rightly the struggle of those identifying as men, too. Even despite male privilege, sexism as a system polices male norms and behaviour and increases pressure upon those men to uphold a status quo. And fixing systemic issues requires systems thinking. Men do not

need to be part of the marginalised group itself to become cognisant of their privileges and role within a system that ultimately harms us all. However, men must understand that genuine allyship, without centring themselves, to women and others who suffer gender inequity is a "rising tide that lifts all boats", with the resulting sea change being one that helps to bring forth a more equitable society for all.'

So ask yourself do you want to make the world a better place for you, for your family, and your friends? If the answer is yes, then that's why you should be a male ally.

Types of allies

Being an ally simply means you are not a member of a particular marginalised or underrepresented group and that you want to support and promote change to this group, which in this case, if you're reading this is women in construction!

I do understand that it is not always easy to be an ally, particularly as some men can become angered by it or become defensive but please don't let that put you off.

It's worth noting here that there are different parts to the journey of being a male ally. This is something Lee Chambers recently posted about on LinkedIn, with a cartoon showing the 'Male Allyship Continuum' journey which shows the various barriers, actions and challenges each stage of the male allyship journey has.[207]

It's important to note that becoming an ally is not a straightforward road and that it will, at times, make you feel uncomfortable, it will challenge you and you will make mistakes on the journey – and that's OK!

In fact you may not have even been aware of some of the issues women faced until you started reading this book. My hope is that having now read some of the experiences women deal with and seen the statistics from the women I have surveyed and spoken to, that you are now curious to know more and open to being part of the solution. After all, the fact some of these issues have been happening since I first started in construction thirty years ago shows how badly we need change.

So what type of ally could you be?

There are seven generally recognised types of ally (based on Karen Catlin's 'Better Allies' process[208]) that you can become and not all of them require you to be publicly waving your ally flag.

1. **The Confidant:** This ally creates an environment that makes people from marginalised/minority groups feel safe enough to share their feelings, needs, frustrations and fears. Importantly this ally provides a listening ear and is not judgemental. They believe these experiences are truthful and they listen, ask questions and provide support.

2. **The Knowledge Seeker/Scholar:** This ally seeks to learn as much as they can about the challenges and prejudices faced by marginalised/minority groups/people. They never insert their own opinions, experiences or ideas; they instead listen and learn. This ally does their own research and will ask co-workers from minority groups about their experiences.

3. **The Sponsor:** This ally openly supports person/s in a minority group aiming to help boost the credibility and reputation of the person/s particularly when they notice situations where the minority person/group is being ignored or dismissed. This could be by talking about them, recommending them and recognising their achievements and expertise to others or by offering development opportunities or practical support, for example.

4. **The Champion:** This ally champions inclusion in public spaces such as industry events, conferences and on social media with the intention of sending a public message to large audiences on the need for equity and inclusivity. This ally may suggest someone from the minority group be included where they have not been or may recommend they speak at an event instead of themselves.

5. **The Amplifier:** This ally works to amplify minority voices to ensure they are heard. This could be by inviting minority groups to speak at meetings, write thought papers or take on other visible roles. It could be as simple as repeating a great idea a minority person had and giving them credit publicly so others see their potential.

6. **The Advocate:** This ally uses their own power or influence to bring underrepresented groups/people into highly exclusive circles by recognising and addressing unjust omissions. This ally will hold their peers accountable to ensure all colleagues are included in these events and activities regardless of their differences.

7. **The Upstander:** This ally is extremely active; they choose not to sit back and watch as a minority group/person is harassed or disrespected. This ally will speak up if someone makes offensive jokes or comments even if no one within earshot may be offended. This ally is not afraid to speak up and fight for the rights of the minority group/person and call out offensive or degrading speech.

What are the barriers to being an ally?

One thing you may notice from the various types of ally is that every single one is an *active* role, whether the actions are in public or private.

But what is it that stops men from becoming allies?

I have spoken to many men about this question in the last few years and I know there are genuine barriers felt by some men when it comes to becoming an ally and putting their head above the proverbial parapet.

In November 2023, I was asked to be on a panel called 'Not All Men' by another gender ally, Jeremy Stockdale. This panel, comprised of three women (myself, Harriet Whaley-Cohen and Kimberley Mezoui), was aimed at men and was to discuss why gender equity benefits everyone. Its goal was to help men see how they could play their part. Jeremy asked us to discuss some of our experiences openly and to explain why it was important for men to be allies to women, and then to take any questions that we were asked.

I not only spoke of my experiences, but I listened hard to the men in the room. We cannot expect men to just become allies to women without understanding some of the things that may hold them back.

I asked my own questions of the men who were there. What was it that concerned them about becoming male allies? I genuinely wanted to know.

I found the experience enlightening as I learned that the main thing holding the men in the room back from being allies to women was not that they didn't care about gender equity, it was in fact fear. Fear of making a mistake, fear of saying the wrong thing and fear of how other men and women may react and judge them.

That evening, I learned that fathers of young men were desperately concerned about the backlash young men were feeling in respect of gender. One man was genuinely scared that his son appeared to hang off every word Andrew Tate says, following him on social media and becoming convinced that gender equality and equity has gone too far. Young men and older men alike are concerned they would somehow be missing out or losing out if women are offered the same opportunities men have had for generations to thrive.

I also learned more about why some men were nervous about allyship and what it means and unsure what they were expected to do.

The fact is, as with anything in life, we don't know what we don't know. It is only by education, lived experience or talking to others that we improve our knowledge.

Becoming an ally isn't always natural and some of the men that evening said they did not know how to start conversations with women who were colleagues (or even friends and family) to ask about lived experiences. They knew they needed to have these conversations so they could understand more about the issues, but they didn't know how to start them.

My comment was simply that by attending this evening they had the perfect opportunity to use that as a start point for a conversation – eg, 'I was at this event last night/week/month and these women were talking about some of their experiences, and I wondered if you had any similar to XYZ.'

If you're a man reading this book you have an ideal opportunity to use this as your 'opener' to having some conversations and listening to the lived experiences of the women around you: 'I just read this book and was wondering X…'

Ask the question, open up the conversation. Women are mostly happy to share and talk about the issues they have faced when asked. Yes there will be some women for whom trauma means they will not want to share, and that's OK, but for the vast majority, asking and showing your genuine interest will more often than not enable an enlightening conversation to start. Then all you need to do is actively listen to what women are saying.

Share your thoughts once you have heard what the women around you at home or work say, ask questions and learn more; most of all, please do have these conversations so we can work together to improve things for all of us.

While fear can be a barrier to learning about the issues and becoming an ally, there are other things you can do if you aren't ready to take that step and have those conversations. There are numerous papers and books out there that can help you to learn more. Follow men on social media who are focused on allyship and inclusion and diversity. As you research more you will find you naturally become more prepared to have conversations on the topic.

The biggest thing to remember is that every one of us can have an impact on making change happen and we can all be allies to each other. If everyone makes small changes, big change is inevitable.

Summary

In this chapter we've looked at the fact that while women are facing numerous issues and need men as allies, the current system is damaging for everyone, aside from a few right at the top who prosper from it.

The patriarchy thrives on the premise that men are dominant and strong and women are weak. However, we have also learned that this same system is causing a huge mental health crisis in men and that compared to the UK national average and other sectors, our industry has a higher rate of mental health problems and suicide in men,[209] whereby we lose two men every working day.[210]

We looked at privilege and why the word is a turn off and instead flipped it to the advantages we have that we may not be aware of. We showed that it is not just the average white man who has advantages over women, for example, but that women can also have advantages over other women and minority groups too.

We have seen why allyship is important and looked at the polarisation where some think women's equality has gone too far compared to those who do not think it has gone far enough. We looked at what allyship means and the various types of ally you can be and how each of them is a proactive role as well as the fact there are barriers men can face when it comes to becoming an ally but that all of us can have an impact and all of us can be allies to each other.

EIGHT
Institutions And Companies, Role Models And Allies – What Can They Do?

In this chapter we are exploring some of the things institutions, companies and people are doing to improve the situation. There are many issues in the industry. Lots is being done to improve things but we need to do more.

This chapter highlights some people who are allies and role models both in the construction industry and beyond who have provided advice for others wanting to start their own journey. The road to being a male ally is not always easy and many men may not have been aware of the issues regularly faced by women and other marginalised groups. This is why sharing these experiences from real women is so important.

I hope that reading the advice and stories from different men will help bring understanding and a sense of teamwork where more men want to engage and become allies to women. Ask yourself, as you read through some of the advice and reasons others have for becoming allies to women and other diverse groups, do I get their why? Can I do that?

It's not just men who need to be allies – women also need to be allies to each other and to men. We know men are also suffering in construction and see this in the mental health and suicide rates, so, while this book is predominantly about making things better for women, I want anyone reading this to understand that being allies to each other, regardless of gender, race, religion or any other points of difference, is imperative to improving the culture in the industry, so that everyone in construction can win.

My wish for this book is that we continue educating ourselves and become the best people we can be, supporting others and standing up against those who choose to harass, intimidate, torment, bully, assault or degrade others. The system is broken and it's up to all of us to fix it.

What are groups and institutions doing to make things better?

There are various institutions, alliances and platforms trying to improve the industry. Not all work being done is specifically related to gender; many are working to improve diversity generally. In this section I highlight some groups and institutions and what they are doing. This is not by any means an exhaustive list and I am sure there will be others out there doing great work to make the industry better.

Building Equality

Building Equality is an alliance of construction consultants, engineers, developers, contractors and institutions working together to drive inclusion for LGBTQIA+ in construction, engineering and the built environment.

www.buildingequalityuk.com

Careers in Construction (CiC)

While not gender-specific, the platform enables companies to recruit candidates and enables candidates to upload CVs and find jobs.

www.careersinconstruction.com

CITB and Supply Chain Sustainability School

In 2023, the results of a survey undertaken by Supply Chain Sustainability School of over 340,000 people in the built environment revealed lack of progress in diversity in all areas (gender, ethnicity and disability).[211] The survey is complemented by an industry-wide Fairness,

Inclusion and Respect (FIR) programme initiative funded and run by the CITB and the Supply Chain Sustainability School, which provides free industry training, workshops, resources and guidance materials that aim to make workplaces better for everyone. This is supported with an Ambassador programme, aiming to support businesses to become more innovative and profitable by dealing with workplace culture challenges and working to attract and retain people.

www.supplychainschool.co.uk

Considerate Constructors Scheme (CCS)

Anyone who works for a contractor will know this institution well. Set up to support the industry in raising standards, being considerate constructors and to build trust with the public. CCS works to encourage considerate practice and provides numerous resources and workshops accessible to all, including women-in-construction e-learning courses designed to educate the sector on the issues women face.

www.considerateconstructors.com

Construction Industry Training Board

The CITB is the industry training board for England, Scotland and Wales sponsored by the Department for Education and accountable to government ministers and parliament. It collects a levy from private firms which is redistributed in industry as part of its role to support a skilled, competent and inclusive workforce.[212] It provides training, grants and education and works on attracting more people into construction.

www.citb.co.uk

Construction Job Board

Again, while not gender-specific, the platform enables companies to recruit candidates and enables candidates to upload CVs and find jobs.

www.constructionjobboard.co.uk

Go Construct

Supported by the CITB levy, Go Construct is an industry-wide initiative and provides resources for those looking for a career in the built environment as well as teachers and careers advisors.

It also provides guidance on organising site visits and work experience as well as a STEM ambassador programme and a yearly skills competition for apprentices and learners raising awareness of the skills and trades available in the industry.

www.goconstruct.org

Home Builders Federation – Women into Home Building Programme

HBF and a network of homebuilders set up this programme to address gender imbalance in the industry. Launched in 2023, the programme helps women to gain careers advice and site management experience and links them with employers to gain jobs and apprenticeships.

www.hbf.co.uk/home-building-skills-partnership/wihb/join

National Association of Women in Construction

This international not-for-profit association is dedicated to the advancement of women in the construction industry, providing support to women in their careers as well as organising site visits, networking events, seminars and workshops and working with industry towards a gender-equal construction industry for the future.

www.nawic.co.uk

National Federation of Builders

The NFB represents builders, contractors and house builders across England and Wales. They offer lots of fully funded training and undertake research, including neurodiversity research. In 2022 they started the Top 100 Women in Construction Awards, aimed at showcasing women in the sector to make female and non-binary role models more visible and accessible. Now they collaborate with CITB in continuing this work to increase visibility, recognise role models and raise the profile of the sector.

www.builders.org.uk

Professional Membership Institutions

In 2022, the following parties (who have a combined membership of over 350,000) collaborated to produce a Memorandum of Understanding to effect meaningful improvement in DEI standards across the built environment:[213] CIOB, Institution of Civil Engineers (www.ice.org.uk), Landscape Institute (www.landscapeinstitute.org), Royal Institute of British Architects (www.architecture.com), RICS (www.rics.org) and Royal Town Planning Institute (www.rtpi.org.uk).

All parties agreed to standardise member data collection, develop information on the transition from education into employment and collate data to understand issues with retention and gaps in education and support the professions by collating and sharing guidance and standards to improve standards across the sectors.

This collaboration is perhaps one of the most important as previously institutions had held and gathered data differently. This standardisation will help the industry measure the situation and work towards a more diverse and inclusive environment.

It is also worth noting that each of these institutes/institutions is separately undertaking their own works in the area of DEI, some of which I have mentioned in this book. I would recommend readers look at each of their websites for further information.

STEMAZING

STEMAZING is a non-profit social enterprise dedicated to inspiration and inclusion in STEM with the purpose of bringing together and amplifying the voices of women in science, technology, engineering and maths.

Set up by Alex Knight to bring more diversity into STEM it has hundreds of role models in various fields including engineering and construction all working together to raise awareness and bring in the next generations. They go into education settings and highlight the varied careers available, including many of those in construction.

www.stemazing.co.uk

Women in The Built Environment (WITBE)

Set up by Shelley Coleman Marsh and Philip Marsh, WITBE is a virtual app-enabled social and mentoring programme to support all women working in the built environment across the globe.

www.knowledgementoring.com/witbe

Women's Engineering Society

WES was founded by members of the National Council of Women during the First World War to campaign for the women who worked in engineering and technical roles during the war to retain them when the war ended. It now promotes engineering for women and works to educate the public about the career opportunities and raise the profile of women engineers. It offers various events, education, mentoring and awards to celebrate and showcase women in engineering.

www.wes.org.uk

What are companies doing and can all of construction emulate?

Are companies doing enough?

There are some great examples of companies changing things to enable men and women to have things like equal leave for child caring. These actions make a huge difference to parents and help challenge traditional 'gender bias'. Rather than women suffering the motherhood penalty, these offerings mean men too can have that time to bond with their children and mothers can, if they choose, go back to work earlier than they perhaps would have been able to had they not been able to share the load.

Here are a few examples of companies (not just in construction) who have instigated changes to help in the fight for fairness.

- Browne Jacobson recently equalised its family policies from two weeks' paternity leave to twenty-six weeks' paternity leave (thirteen weeks fully paid and thirteen weeks at half pay), also offering the same for co-parents and adoption leave.

- Aviva has some family-friendly offerings like equal parental leave, offering new parents up to twelve months' leave with six months at full basic pay; since 2018, almost half of the people who had taken leave were men.[214] This leave is applicable to birth, adoption and surrogate parents and if both parents work for Aviva they each have entitlement which they can take at the same time.

- Spotify recently confirmed that it was continuing to offer its employees fully remote working, unlike companies like Amazon and Dell and various tech companies who have recently instigated return to work for most employees five days a week. Spotify's Chief of HR, Katarine Berg, said there has been no impact on productivity or efficiency and, while they are investigating making collaboration easier in a virtual environment, Spotify is a business 'that's been digital from birth, so why shouldn't we give our people flexibility and freedom?' She said, 'Work is not a place you come to, it's something you do.'[215] Unsurprisingly, allowing its employees to work from anywhere has also led to a drop in its attrition rates by 15%.

- Duolingo achieved a 50% ratio of women new engineering college hires in 2018 by changing its strategy in a number of ways. It recruited from colleges with more than the US average women enrolled, networked with women's groups at colleges, sponsored the 2017 Grace Hopper conference, ensured its women engineers attended and instigated interviewer unconscious bias training and had women on interview panels.

- HS2 brought in 'blind auditioning' instead of CVs, where an anonymous technical assessment is completed for the first stage.[216] This increased applicant success rates for women in short listing by over 50%.

- Wates overhauled its family-friendly policies in 2020, enhancing their parental leave policy (increasing fully paid paternity leave from eight weeks to twelve weeks and making their maternity, shared parental leave and adoption and surrogacy policies a day-one entitlement) and enhancing the carers leave policy (to be applicable from day one of employment). They also introduced flexible working policies, encouraging this at all roles in the business (something that was mentioned a few times in my survey by the women who work at Wates). In their work to address bullying, harassment and discrimination, Wates filmed professional actors playing out experiences that had been the subject of investigation in their business.[217] After being shocked by the film, the leadership team produced a group pledge and built a Charter to ensure such issues do not continue, with everyone expected to help eradicate bad behaviours.

- Kier undertook an audit in 2021 with external support to assess D&I in the organisation and subsequently created a five-year plan to develop.[218] Since then Kier has re-launched its employee networks, instituted family-friendly policies,[219] D&I education, reverse mentoring, D&I targets for all managers, inclusive recruitment policies, various employee support policies (menopause, fertility, domestic abuse, etc), inclusion champions and agile working on site. Kier in 2022 confirmed they had seen a 20% rise in applicants since they had introduced family-friendly policies. One of these was increased paid maternity leave to twenty-six weeks with no qualifying period for this to kick in. They also introduced a carers policy with five days' paid leave for those with caring needs,[220] as well as a returners scheme to entice those who had been on a career break to come back to the industry.[221]

- Laing O'Rourke introduced at least six months' parental leave at full pay with no waiting period in 2022, followed by other family policies (eg phased returns to work and a pregnancy loss policy).[222] In 2024, they also introduced their Gender Equality Action Plan setting out how they will achieve leading gender parity targets.[223]

- Transport for London (TfL) has recognised that flexibility is key. Some people work mostly from home, others do a hybrid version spending a day or two in the office, and others do compressed hours with ten days compressed into nine so they can have an extra day off. The main thing is the culture of having respect for people. As long as deadlines are met, they work collaboratively with staff and supply chain. Even station staff can work flexibly. The other thing TfL has done is to fix core hours to be between 10am and 2pm rather than 9am and 5pm. This enables people with caring responsibilities to be in meetings, for example.[224]

There are others out there doing good things, but I can't list them all here due to space constraints. There are also companies who say they are doing good things yet in my survey the women working there said it's actually the polar opposite based on their experience. This tells us there is a real need to ensure continuous measurement by way of safe employee surveys run by external independent companies as without these some companies may be unaware of how the women working for them really feel.

In 2021 a pioneer programme co-designed by Timewise and Build UK, with support from Barclays Life Skills programme and CITB, was piloted.[225] Four leading construction firms took part (BAM Construct, BAM Nuttall, Skanska UK and Willmott Dixon), trialling specific working patterns on site, with various options from staggered start and finish times to flexi day approaches with differing hours from those contracted.

All firms involved reported that flexible working *had no negative impact on budgets or timeframes* and data showed there were some savings on labour costs due to increased productivity.

So it's clear the industry is missing a trick if it is choosing not to use flexible working. Timewise also provided a 10-point plan, which can be used by anyone who wants to pilot flexible working themselves.[226]

Infrastructure Matters released the 'Women in Infrastructure' report in 2023 following research in that sector.[227] The report provides various best practice case studies that others can emulate to assist them in improving gender diversity practices.

Work with men to help them be allies

While I have covered some of the issues around gender equality in Chapter 2 and we know there are fewer women in positions of power globally, the question for me was how do we engage the men around us and in power to help improve gender inequality in construction? After all it is the people in power who can lead from the top and help change culture and behaviours.

A few years ago former Australian Sex Discrimination Commissioner (2007–2015) Elizabeth Broderick established a 'Champions of Change' coalition whereby she set about persuading some of Australia's top CEOs to lead on DEI.[228] She engaged over 260 CEOs and their organisations and did this by making it personal. She shared real stories, and when the men in power listened to these real-life stories, they started to realise the inequities women were facing. One of the CEOs she spoke to had recently had twins, a girl and a boy. Elizabeth simply asked did he realise his daughter would never get the same opportunities her twin brother would.

But not everyone is a parent, and some men with daughters may not even consider the inequalities she will face until she's older… maybe the first time as a teenage girl she's cat called on the street, for example.

This is why listening to people's stories is important as it helps others to understand the issues faced. This book has stories from many women ranging in age from eighteen through to seventy.

I asked a few questions of the women who took my survey in specific reference to DEI policies and the results were interesting:

Question	Yes	No	Maybe/Not applicable
As businesses set DEI targets and gender balance targets, do you think enough is being done to really address the key issues and empower women, change company policies and do more than simply paying lip service to the issues?	19.87%	79.47%	0.66%[229]
Do you think policies to help DEI actually work?	16.89%	19.54%	63.58%
Do you think specific gender policies can alienate men in the workplace?	61.59%	37.75%	0.66%

In fact things didn't improve through this section of the survey and an overwhelming 63% of women felt DEI policies mean women are taken less seriously, as men think they only got the job to tick the diversity box.

We know this is reflected in the global research that is currently showing the pushback against DEI that is being encountered because many men feel alienated and left out.

So how can we tackle this?

This is where education and understanding is really important. We need to ensure men do not feel this way and, moreover, ensure that men know that women getting more equality does not take anything away from men; in fact, everyone will win as the culture will change for the better for everyone. As Lee Chambers likes to say when he talks about diversity, more diversity doesn't mean less pie for men, it means more pie and more choice of pie for everyone.

This is where allyship is important if we are to make a difference to the industry, to the numbers of women and other diverse groups coming into it and to the retention of those already within it.

Male role models and allies in construction

Equality needs men as allies and in my research 67% of women understand that's not an easy thing to do. A large part of this book is about how everyone needs to work together to make change happen. My career has not always been easy, as you may have gathered from some of the stories I have shared, but I wouldn't be here now if it wasn't for some amazing and supportive role models. I have spoken to many men for the book and have selected a few of them to provide their advice and/or their why.

Why should we want to improve things not just for the construction industry, but for all of us, and what can you do if you are reading this today that will make a difference from tomorrow?

Richard Whitehead

I met Richard Whitehead (Chief Executive, Global Buildings & Places at AECOM) in 2022 speaking on a panel about male allies. One of the things I loved was the fact that he acknowledged he sometimes finds it hard to be a male ally. He didn't and doesn't always know what to do but his underlying value is his big sense of fairness. He believes any sort of disadvantage because someone is a different gender is unfair. Richard's advice to other men who may want to become an ally but are unsure where to start is this:

> 'Don't be frightened. Yes, it takes courage but it's the little things that add up. Work to get rid of your own bias, we all have it, and it takes conscious effort and openness to change it… Ask people around you to give you feedback and tell you if something you say isn't quite right so this is brought into your awareness and you can alter it in the future.'

Richard realises being an ally also has an impact on other men as they see fairness from him is important and this in turn can help others change their views and behaviours.

When we discussed the fact that men are sometimes concerned that women get the job over them just to hit D&I targets, he was very clear: 'I have never promoted someone because they are a woman, it just wouldn't be sensible. There will be men who lose out on jobs, yes, but that will be because they just weren't as good as the women candidates in that instance.'

Reaching equality and equity is not about disadvantaging someone else; this is a common misconception. Equity means creating the right circumstances and giving people the tools they need to do the job well whoever they may be regardless of age, gender or race.

David Savage

I have known David for many years, having first met him on seminars he used to run out of the Guildford office. He's a Partner in Charles Russell Speechlys LLP, and he's not just a great construction lawyer but also a real inspiration when it comes to his allyship. When I asked his advice for others looking to venture on the road to allyship he said:

> 'Showing allyship demonstrates not just support to women working in our industry, but also that men have understood the strategic significance of the positive change that is happening, needs to continue to

happen, and will happen anyway. Allyship is the catalyst to make that change happen faster. And given that change is urgently needed in the construction sector, allyship matters enormously.'

Bob Cummings

In 2022, I attended Bob's talk at the NEC People Conference. Bob, a former civil engineer and health and safety professional, is now a behavioural engineer focused on culture change. I particularly enjoyed his explanation of how simple association techniques can help people change – humans generally prefer to be linked to something positive rather than negative.

He explained that we see the world through our past experiences, which shape our current reality. We're bound by these experiences until new ones change our perspective. Rather than getting frustrated by others' views, we should approach them with curiosity and empathy, considering what experiences have led them to their opinions.

I've included many comments from women in this book to show the challenges they face. As Bob pointed out, when we understand how our actions affect others, we can associate negative feelings with harmful behaviour, enabling learning and change, even in those who may have acted poorly.

Gary Mumford

Gary was an awesome boss to have in my early career as he was always fair. His childhood had a lot to do with that; he had a dad who believed in giving people a chance and a mum who had been a childminder to a Nigerian boy when they were young and who'd instilled into him, and his brothers, that this boy was to be treated as one of the family and like another brother and they were to stand up against any prejudice that may come from others towards him or them. They did get some and I think these experiences shaped him and are part of the reason why he was always so fair.

When I asked him about what other men on the allyship journey could do he said, 'Always give people a chance. Everyone deserves an opportunity so never pre-judge or be prejudiced. Remember, we can all have biases, so do things to stop it.'

He gave an example about recruiting:

'If interviewing, remove any potential for bias. Have mixed panels and get agencies to send CVs with just the facts (ie qualifications and experience only, no names, dates or other personal data) to ensure there is nothing that may influence you and you are only looking at the person's qualifications and experience. A 50-year-old that is brilliant at the job but doesn't want promotion should not be overlooked because of a lack of ambition. Don't discount people based on your own bias or prejudices.'

James Flemming

I met James at the 2023 Women in Construction Awards and what struck me about James was his passion to make things better. An engineer who previously worked in oil and gas and became involved in DEI when he moved roles, James noticed that women often outshone men in terms of focus, commitment and energy yet were not having that turn into promotion. He set up a fast-track system giving women a clear path to promotion at all levels and noticed they excelled. Since then, he and his wife have set up a motivational intelligence company offering leadership training and a programme specifically for women in construction to give them new solutions to the challenges they face.[230] He is now working on a course specifically for men to educate them about the issues women face and to help them on their allyship journey.

James is a male ally who wants to stop women from being frightened to speak up and to educate men on the impact the words they say can have on women. His advice to men is, 'Other men need to be held accountable so call it out. It's not down to women; men need to take action.'

Steffan Battle

I have known Steffan a long time, having worked with him at Wates many years ago. During the process of writing the book he became Executive Managing

INSTITUTIONS AND COMPANIES, ROLE MODELS AND ALLIES

Director of Wates Construction and I know his active allyship can only ever improve the culture and I have no doubt he will make a big difference to staff. I asked him about what other men can do to be better allies to women and other marginalised or minority groups in construction and he said:

> 'If you hear something and do nothing you are also culpable. If you see it you have to call it out. Allyship is active and you can have a huge impact on others in a powerful and positive way. Use a model like the "Active Bystander model" to intervene safely if you aren't sure. Do not sit by and do nothing when someone is not being treated right, we must intervene to show the wrongdoer that the behaviour is unacceptable.'

So what is this model? It's simple and effective and has various ways to use it depending on the scenario:

1. **Direct action:** Call out the negative behaviour in a calm way. Ask the person to stop or ask the victim if they are OK openly.

2. **Distract:** Interrupt or start a conversation with the perpetrator to allow the potential target to move away or find a way to get the victim out of the situation.

3. **Delegate:** If you don't feel comfortable speaking out or don't feel safe have someone else step in.

4. **Delay:** If the situation is dangerous in some way or you feel outnumbered, walk away and wait; report it and ask the victim later if they are OK. It's never too late to act.

We discussed Steffan's 'why' and it was simple from his perspective:

> 'If you understand your own privilege, you become aware of your impact. We often don't know the privilege we have over others and the word can get some people's backs up; however, when we accept it, we can collaborate and advocate for others. It's the decent thing to do and it is the way to improve things for everyone.'

Andy Beard

I worked with Andy briefly at Arcadis and one thing I loved about working with him was his empathy for others. He doesn't judge people and when we spoke about what other men could do to be better allies to women, he said simply:

> 'Put yourself in other people's shoes and use your empathy to imagine how you would feel if it was you or your spouse or child or friend dealing with the situation. No one has the right to make others feel bad so stand up for others who may be unable to do so themselves in

that moment. That's what allyship is, helping others and improving culture as a result.'

Chris Moran

There are all sorts of ways to be an ally, but each requires positive action. I was introduced to Chris Moran thanks to Marion Ellis. Previously a police officer for fifteen years, Chris moved into construction and was awarded the RICS Surveyors Matrics Residential Surveyor of the Year 2024. He has a passion to improve diversity in the industry and set up the Moran-Amaral Foundation, a twelve-session programme run over six months to provide technical training, mentoring and experience to students to enable them to progress, and part of the pledge they sign states that after graduation and when they have a year's post-qualification experience, they will in turn mentor three students from an underrepresented background.

Chris is a great example of how we can make a difference to others. When we spoke he told me how when he was nominated he had a table and decided to invite someone who would otherwise not have been represented to enable them to network and be seen. He posted on LinkedIn and had two women quantity surveyors help him choose the winner from the applications and he paid all travel and hotel costs to ensure there was nothing that would prevent them from being able to attend. Giving others a place at the table is so important and enables them to be seen!

Pete Wilder

While not a direct quote I spoke to Pete and also his wife Sara having seen him speak at the RICS about how they had chosen to share childcare responsibilities. He was open about some of the issues men can face from others (mostly men) when they can't attend a meeting if they are collecting children or taking them to the dentists, for example. His advice that day, to men listening, was to talk about the caring more to help normalise it, to remember if the work is done there should be no issue and to move and find a safe environment if the place you are working in is not supportive to your needs.

Richard Thorpe

I spoke to ex-colleague Richard Thorpe about allyship as he has led many high-performing and diverse teams, and his name came up a few times during my research. Richard looks at things from a different perspective and asks simply what is the pathway to a successful team?

Over the years he has honed his method and, when we discussed it, what became apparent is his intrinsic sense of fairness and the fact he wants to create trust and a caring culture where everyone can be themselves. He has seen the high performance and innovation that's created when he has a balance of men and women, but it goes further than this. Richard works on the culture, creating work spaces that work for women, he looks at different working practices to accommodate caring responsibilities and ensures everyone is aware of the various support mechanisms available to them. Most importantly he creates teams where successes are celebrated equally for men and women and promotes open discussion. People feel safe, knowing they will get support and training and most importantly that poor behaviour is not tolerated.

Noel McKee

I met Noel through the Women in Construction Hub set up by Michaela Wain. He is a male ally who has spent time listening to women in the hub, learning and asking questions and working to understand the issues women face in the industry. I asked Noel what he thought other men should do and he said men need to advocate more and think before they speak. He went on to say:

> 'Men need to step out of the shadows and not care what people say. Ask the questions, give advice and encouragement, be willing to change and most of all realise that we all have a duty of care for the people around us to ensure they feel valued and cared for. Construction is a people industry, without the people we have nothing, just remember that everyone you work with is somebody's child, so support, care and lead by example in everything.'

Liam Holder

Liam is Managing Director at Secretariat and when it came to being an ally to women, he was mentioned a few times in the survey responses from various women who have worked with him over the years. I asked Liam what his 'why' was for being an ally to women and he gave me this brilliant list:

- 'I have been in many boardrooms and operated in "top tier" management groups for a number of years – I have been constantly embarrassed at the lack of women in those rooms. It isn't just women either of course.

- I have worked with many women over the years – both reporting to them and also women reporting to me. I have rarely been less than impressed.

- Two of the best leaders I have ever worked for are women.

- Some of the best lawyers/counsel I have ever worked with are women.

- The companies where women appeared to have a higher profile were better places to work.

- I have three daughters.

- Men are not better, cleverer, harder-working etc than women so why the imbalance?

- I dislike injustice and I dislike hurdles being put in your way – it took a pandemic to change most businesses' attitudes towards flexible working – which hitherto had I think been a major barrier to women's career progression.

- I could go on…'

Then we have male role models who are openly and proudly shouting from the proverbial rooftop their support for inclusivity in the industry.

Danny Clarke CMIOSH

Danny is a huge advocate of inclusivity in construction and if you follow him on LinkedIn you will know he regularly discusses this in his posts.[231] Head of Engagement with the CITB and instigator of the Top 100 Women in Construction Awards, Danny's passion to make the industry a better place is infectious. When we spoke about the specific topic of allyship and why it's important, he said:

> 'Allyship, particularly male allyship, is an essential element of achieving gender equality and creating a more inclusive society. By recognising and using their position and in some cases privilege, male allies are able to constructively challenge gender-based discrimination and support women and non-binary individuals in their professional

lives. It's important to me because promoting gender equality is crucial for creating a just and equitable society where everyone is able to thrive.

'Male allyship also inspires other men to take action and help them break down harmful societal norms and beliefs that perpetuate gender inequality. In short, male allyship is essential in the fight for gender equality and can create a more supportive and inclusive world for everyone.'

Chirag Shah FIRP

As part of my research I have had some amazing men step up during the process to help me. One of these is Chirag Shah, a project controls expert and founder of PACE Global.

When we discussed male allyship, one of the things that came up was the need for male allies to understand better how they can help women. This can be simple things like speaking up when women are spoken over or their views are ignored in meetings. Chirag said:

'There needs to be better education and initiative taken by all to educate ourselves on gender inequality and unconscious bias. We should proactively reach out to women and listen and learn to their experiences and concerns in the workplace.'

Chirag said he was:

> '… proactively seeking female leaders who can be mentors in Project Controls, so they can guide the next generation to succeed. I also think as males we should reach out to females and offer to use our position and influence to advocate for their professional development and more importantly promoting their visibility.'

One of the things Chirag is passionate about is the need for companies to properly support women, particularly when it comes to returning to work post pregnancy, for example.

His view is that keeping-in-touch days pre-return and mentored fast-track returns should be used to bring women up to speed and ensure they are quickly reintegrated into the team. Promotions should not be put on hold; if someone's good enough and doing the work they should be promoted regardless of whether they have had time away or not. He said:

> 'This would help reduce the gender pay gap as often women fall further behind after starting a family due to the antiquated notion that because they have been away they are somehow less worthy of promotion and need to wait another year.'

Male role models and advice from outside of the industry

As part of my research into male allyship I spoke to men both inside and outside the construction industry, so let's look at those who aren't in construction next and see how other industries may tackle the equality issue with role models and allies.

First, here are a few famous public ones, really providing great examples to other men of what allyship looks like.

In sport my first is one of my favourites, tennis player Andy Murray, as he has consistently shown his allyship to women publicly. In 2017, he calmly corrected a reporter who said Sam Querrey was the first American player to make it to a major semi-final since 2009 by simply deadpan saying 'male player', pointing out that women American players had achieved that feat more recently.[232]

Then we have football, with Ian Wright, a male ally passionate about the women's game, loudly speaking out about the challenges they face and the inequity in how women in the game and women pundits are treated because of men.[233] Harry Redknapp and Jermaine Jenas joined Heineken's campaign in 2022, '12th Woman', showing their support for the women's game.[234]

Rugby player Ugo Moyne regularly speaks out about male allyship[235] and how sport should not have a gender.[236]

If we look at other famous people we have people like Ryan Gosling, John Legend, David Schwimmer,

Benedict Cumberbatch, Barack Obama, Antonio Guterres, Justin Trudeau.

There are many male allies publicly supporting women and women's rights, yet as we have seen throughout the book globally women's rights have actually gone backwards. This is why it is so important we work together to stop this reversal. Part of that means working together and not pushing men away.

I hope it is clear throughout this book that while I am passionate about making things better for women that does not mean at the expense of men. I want things to be better for us all, but that means we need to have more male allies help us get gender equality back on track.

I have spoken to a number of men who work consistently to be allies to women and to challenge people's thinking, and there were too many to have all of them in this book. I have therefore selected a few who have provided advice, their why or are people other men can follow so that they too can get on the journey to being an ally.

Let's start in the world of sport.

Gregg Bateman

Gregg is an ex-professional rugby player I saw speak in 2022 at an Inspiring Women in Construction Conference and found his ethos around mental health and teamwork really inspiring.

As part of the research into allyship, I wanted to know what he thought when it comes to becoming a male ally to women and us all working together for the greater good. The first thing he said was:

> 'It's really f****** difficult and I honestly don't know the answer, but I am happy to go on the journey and be open minded. Sadly, when you talk about privilege, the most common response is likely to be guilt, or "should I feel guilty" and then you get defensiveness; the other side of that is empathy.
>
> 'So, I guess, it's about choosing to look at it through a lens of empathy rather than a lens of guilt though because the patriarchal issues that have left some having advantages over others are not of our making today, they are historical. It's also important, I suppose to provide the pathway to understanding, so show and demonstrate *how* men can understand the differences first. That's how I would be engaged: show me the injustice and I'll get in your corner and fight for it with you.'

Gregg's attitude is that he wants to know what it's like to walk in someone else's shoes so that he can make informed decisions. He wants to be invited to come on the journey so he has the opportunity to understand the issues, discuss them openly in a safe space and come to his own self-realisation.

This is what all of us can do, work together to create a safe space for us to all work together fairly.

Scott Ward MBA

Scott is an ex-footballer who debuted for Luton at eighteen and played for other clubs including Coventry City and Crawley Town but injury halted his career.

I also saw him speak at the 2022 Inspiring Women in Construction Conference and his passion to help others and be an ally to women was clear.

He's CEO and founder of Humanise Solutions and, from his years of research, he has designed and delivered multiple initiatives, including a 'Young Adult Personal Development Programme' and a City and Guilds certified ILM Women's Leadership Programme.[237]

His involvement in the leadership programme comes from his understanding of the unique issues many women face and his passion to help. He said, 'Being a male ally is important but so is assisting women by development opportunities delivered in a safe environment. Women on this programme will get coaching, tools and resources to help them in their careers.'

While I don't believe we need to 'fix women' we do need to give women the opportunity to grow and improve their skills. The ILM programme developed by Scott builds on his passion to be an ally to women and provides a safe environment for women to develop and grow.

Outside the world of sport there are people like Robert Baker, Daniele Fiandaca and Lee Chambers.

Robert Baker

I spoke to Robert Baker, a huge advocate of allyship programmes, to help build diverse, equitable and inclusive workplaces, having followed him for a long while on LinkedIn. When we spoke about my industry and my wish to get more men to become allies to women, Robert shared the research he had done with his business partner Daniele Fiandaca in 2022.[238]

The research underlined five things that had been a key trigger for men becoming more involved in inclusion and diversity efforts:

1. Knowing what it is like to be in the outgroup

2. Being a father of girls

3. Recognising their own privilege

4. Sense of injustice

5. It's the right thing to do

It also found men were leaning into D&I efforts at different rates with some doing what the researchers considered to be the bare minimum while others were going beyond this by being allies or agents of change. The research is really interesting, and I particularly like the 'Men Leaning In Matrix' which clearly details the different types of activity and where this sits (Leaning In, Allies or Agents of Change) and can help men to see things they can start doing to make a difference.

Finding out men's why was one of the top tips to getting men involved with D&I efforts and that is why

I have spoken to men inside the industry as well as outside. I want this to help inspire men reading this.

The research also identified the same thing I mentioned in Chapter 7: there is genuine fear.

Robert's advice to other men is to take some simple actions. Speak to women and other minorities about their career and the issues they may have faced, think about your own bias and undertake the Harvard Implicit Bias Test and come from a place of curiosity.

Daniele Fiandaca

I had been following Daniele Fiandaca on LinkedIn for some time. He is a cofounder of Token Man, keynote speaker and founder of Token Man Consulting (a consultancy which specialises in engaging senior leaders and men with the DEI strategy, inspiring them to become allies and agents of change, thus creating more inclusive, diverse, equitable and accessible workplaces). He is also a cofounder of Masculinity in The Workplace, one of very few events with a majority male attendance, accompanied by an annual survey to measure how masculine workplaces continue to be in the UK.

Daniele entered the diversity space having been the only male at a dinner with thirteen women, which made him realise just how difficult it was to be in the outgroup. A conversation with Emma Perkins off the back of this experience happened soon after. As he made mistakes when talking about gender equality, he noticed that she didn't judge him but instead asked him questions that made him think, and that led to him becoming more educated and eventually launching the Token Man Initiative in 2014 with Emma, Georgia Barretta and Penny Othen. They recognised that historically no minority had ever affected change without the support of the majority and Token Man was born as a platform to engage those in the majority.

When we spoke about male allyship Daniele agreed that education is key:

> 'Education is a huge part of becoming an ally and one of the best things men can do is put themselves into an "out" group. So go to a women's group or an LGBTQIA+ group and listen. This helps you to identify the absence of barriers you may have when compared to other minorities.'

However, if men aren't comfortable doing this there are other ways to start the journey. Daniele's advice on this was to 'Go into it gently. Read books and educate yourself. Get used to not speaking. Listen. Find brave spaces to have conversations. Most of all remember it takes time.'

Lee Chambers

Lee is a British psychologist, author, male ally and speaker and the founder of Male Allies UK and Essentialise Workplace Wellbeing. Lee is passionate about inclusive leadership, male allyship and menopause awareness.

Lee is incredibly inspiring; I would urge anyone who wants to be an ally or become a better ally to follow him on LinkedIn.[239]

There are so many gender stereotypes that are damaging to society. For example we know women are often seen as the default caregiver and men as the provider and that men are often discriminated against if they want to be more involved with their children.

Lee became a stay-at-home dad in 2015 after illness and it was during this time he started to learn more about the issues women faced. He listened to conversations in toddler groups and asked questions and started to realise some of the problems women face.

Lee writes about allyship regularly, and when we spoke one of the first things he said was 'Allyship takes time and effort to apply. Allyship is uncomfortable and it should be as uncomfortable as the marginalized feel.'

We dug into this a little more and discussed how many men have been turned off by the use of the word 'privilege' which has become seen as more of a trigger or attack by some men, as noted in Chapter 7. We also discussed the different exercises people can do (such as the BBC's 'Ally Track') so that even the most privileged can see that even they have been excluded from something, like the rugby or football team at school.

Lee said:

'We need to get people to realise that some people feel excluded every single day. Men need to learn about these issues. The more you learn about the issues women and other minorities suffer the more you start to see things that are hidden in plain sight based on the way society has been built.'

One of the biggest hurdles I have noticed when discussing allyship with men in the research for my book is that many men do not know what it means to be an ally or what they can personally do. Men have been conditioned from a young age 'to fix it' but the fact is women do not want a white knight in shining armour to come and fix things. We want men to take a step back and listen to the issues and work with us to change them.

Lee's journey has taught him a lot and it is ongoing and his suggestions for men to start on their ally journey are as follows:

- Don't be fearful. It is not men versus women; it's about having the best of men and the best of women.

- Allyship is the leadership skill of the future – you have to be loud and active enough to create ripples and get other men engaged.

- You need to know when to decentre yourself and move yourself out of the way to bring women forward.

- Sponsorship is an important part of allyship – champion women even when they are not there and role model these behaviours to other men.

- Speak to other men who are a few steps ahead in their allyship journey; you can learn a lot from other men.

- Be committed and know it's a journey and you won't always get it right and that's OK.

Stewart Codling

There are bad men everywhere – construction, banking, the police, the fire service, the NHS, across all industries. *However, it's not all men*, and we need to recognise that. When I spoke to Stewart, Chief Inspector of Thames Valley Police, he said:

> 'Some men will use humour or banter and not realise they are being disrespectful. Men need to be educated and learn to be more thoughtful and take a step back and remember that most men don't fear sexual assault or regular harassment the way women (and minorities) do.
>
> 'I'd recommend going to YouTube and watching Poppy Murray's poem she read post Sarah Everard's murder which explains just this, because while it's not all men, it is all women.[240]
>
> 'Don't be scared to be an ally. This is why education of yourself is key. I haven't lost anything by being an ally; in fact I have better and different conversations with my kids, my family, friends and colleagues that I never would have had before. These conversations sow seeds. Seeds grow and make change happen and as a collective our voice is stronger.'

James Coomber

James spent over twenty years working for the fire service and now provides coaching and training to challenge and change toxic behaviour in the workplace. He is passionate about inclusivity and creating behavioural shifts to provide safe working environments where people can thrive.

I met him through a mutual connection on LinkedIn when I was talking about the importance of male allyship, and I asked him what other men can do to become better allies to women. He said:

> 'Men need to learn about the issues women face. We don't know everything but if we deepen our understanding, we can become better allies. Listen to the women around you and "hear" their experiences. Don't immediately offer advice, just listen and ask questions so you learn more. If you see a situation that is not right, remember as an ally you need to speak up, but do it in a nice way. It's not about shaming other people; we can all educate and learn from each other.'

Sal Naseem FRSA

I spoke to Sal having followed him on LinkedIn for some time. Sal, a South Asian Muslim who grew up in the 1970s and '80s and experienced abuse from racism, is passionate about allyship, not just in respect of race or religion but also when it comes to women and other marginalised groups. Sal spent a decade working in the police misconduct system at the Independent Office for Police Conduct (IOPC) and as a result he understands a lot about male violence against women and girls.

When we spoke about allyship he said how important it is to remember it's a journey and for men to see that it is on all men to fix the issues women face. He said it should not be incumbent on women and girls to end violence and misogyny against them, just as it isn't incumbent on him as a person of colour to lead the change on the fight against racism. He reiterated this on a LinkedIn post and explained the importance of men leading the change.[241]

We also discussed the importance of not 'bashing' men (or indeed anyone) when it comes to trying to create allies. If we do that, we simply create defensiveness. Instead it's about the small changes we can all make to be allies to each other. We need to be educating ourselves and Sal recommended two sources for men to start their allyship journey:

- HeForShe, the UN Global Solidarity Movement for Gender Equality, which has resources and solutions men can immediately use – www.heforshe.org/en

- White Ribbon, the UK's leading charity engaging men and boys to end violence against women and girls – www.whiteribbon.org.uk

While not everything is physical violence, the sexism and misogyny, harmful attitudes, systems and behaviours women face perpetuate inequality and violence. These resources can help men understand the issues and step forward into allyship.

Dheeraj Bhasin MBE

Dheeraj was for seventeen years the only Indian fighter pilot in the RAF. The son of parents who came to the UK in 1966, he started his cadet training in 1980 and has an impressive CV of experience in the military. As a minority, Dheeraj faced a lot of bias. He joined the BAME (Black, Asian and Minority Ethnic) steering group in the RAF but said he later resigned as he felt nothing was changing.

We spoke about how often he had dealt with bias in the RAF and his concerns when people do not educate themselves. His advice to others is that we all have bias but if something is brought into your awareness and you do not alter your behaviour, it then becomes conscious bias and that is a problem.

Oliver Lee OBE

Oliver was in the Royal Marines and since the Marines has held various leadership positions. He is known to promote diversity while transforming culture. Oliver has also faced challenges, and he is vulnerable and open about them and how they have made him stronger.

I spoke to him about how we can encourage everyone, particularly men, to come on this journey and work to make the culture better for everyone. He said, 'Few things are more valuable than generating truly inclusive workplaces. The journey is not always easy, requiring courage and conviction, but the destination is magical.'

These words really resonate. Construction can be magical when we look at what we can create, so why not create an equally magical culture in which everyone can thrive!

Jeremy Stockdale

As mentioned in Chapter 7, I have known Jeremy for a few years. For me he's a great example of an ally because I have watched Jeremy grow into his allyship since I met him. He doesn't always get it right (let's face it none of us do) and sometimes people challenge him, but he continues to show up and learn and educate others with his work and every week with his posts.

Sometimes being an ally is putting yourself out there to help others. It's accepting you won't always get it right and it's about self-reflection and having the strength to be challenged. This applies no matter who you are.

This book is not about lambasting those who have had it easier than others; it is about creating awareness so that we can all make changes for the better to create a fairer and more equitable industry so that everyone in construction can win.

What can male allies do specifically?

One of the things many have asked as I have written this book over the past few years is 'OK, what can I do?' I have collated a number of things that anyone reading this as a potential male ally can do, starting immediately, now you know some of the issues women and other diverse groups are facing daily.

Here are a few examples of situations where you as a male ally (or indeed anyone as an ally) can do something specific to make change happen.

Situation: *You are in a meeting and someone continually speaks over or interrupts the woman at the table.*
Action: Notice the interruption and then say, 'Hold on there X; I think Faye had a point to make there.'

Situation: *A woman makes a point in a meeting but it quickly gets lost.*
Action: Amplify it: 'Faye just said that actually X and it's a fantastic idea; lets discuss it further.'

Situation: *You are in a meeting and the woman at the table isn't being included in the meeting but you know she has expertise.*
Action: Proactively and positively bring her in: 'I'd really like to hear what Faye has to say as she's a subject matter expert.'

Situation: *You see a woman being cat called or whistled at.*

Action: Go to the men doing the cat calling / whistling and tell them the remarks / behaviours are not appropriate or acceptable.

Situation: *A woman confides in you that she's upset about a sexist comment/experience she has had.*
Action: First, say, 'I believe you.' Second, ask her to tell you more about what happened, and actively listen. Finally, if she asks your advice, then talk. Do not say: 'Oh, it was just a joke / that's just how he is / don't take it personally / he's a good bloke / [insert your excuse here]'. This undermines the woman and what she is feeling.

Situation: *You are at a networking event where women are in the minority.*
Action: Introduce women you know there to others. These events are uncomfortable for many people, especially if they are in the minority, so make the effort to ensure women (and others) are included. Even when the woman is not in the room, there are actions you can take as an ally.

Situation: *You're chatting with colleagues and the name of another colleague, who is a woman, comes up (or doesn't).*
Actions: Praise the woman to other colleagues. Advocate for colleagues who are women to get opportunities. Champion and endorse women for leadership positions. Celebrate accomplishments of the women you work with.

Situation: *You're on a team responsible for a public event or publication.*
Actions: Share your influence, knowledge and resources. Put women up to speak at events or to write papers that will help them get opportunities.

Situation: *You're in a board meeting or a yearly review management meeting.*
Action: Advocate for equal pay.

Situation: *You're in a communal space with only men and you hear sexist comments.*
Action: Do not accept sexist comments or language. Call it out. If you do not call it out among other men, then there is an assumption from everyone present that it's OK.

The list is by no means exhaustive, but it gives a flavour of some of the small things you can do to start the process.

The biggest thing men can do is keep learning and most of all remember being an ally is not about you. Research shows men like actions and want to 'fix' but it's not about you fixing things or speaking for women.

Another thing I wanted to do as part of this book was ensure that men know they have the support of women when making the journey into allyship. We know it's not easy but the women involved in my research also had some advice for you which I hope will help, in response to the following question.

'What would you say to a man who wants to become an ally if he is concerned about making a mistake?'

'Ask the women you are working with what they need from you and your allyship, listen and learn.'

'We will all make mistakes when trying to change, when learning about something new. The situation is always fluctuating too so ask questions, be open to feedback, and do whatever you can with good intentions.'

'Mistakes are OK if we can see you are at least trying. Sometimes it really is the thought that counts. If you are supportive, we will appreciate it, even if you do something daft.'

'It's OK to feel uncomfortable about it, uncomfortable is the only way to realise how women/minorities feel and move on.'

'If you are being supportive and it is coming from a place of wanting to help, you can't go too wrong. Where mistakes are made, they should be learned from – speak to those needing your allyship – ask them how they want it to look.'

'The intention to be an ally means a lot. Nobody is perfect and mistakes are made. Please don't be

> disheartened or discouraged, your support is so valuable in making real change.'

I'm sure you can see the theme here: women know mistakes will be made and that's OK, so don't let that put you off from the journey of being an ally!

Summary

In this chapter we have taken a look at the work that some groups and institutions have done and are doing, along with companies both in and outside the construction industry, to improve things for women and we have seen how this benefits everyone!

In making wholesale changes to improve things for women and other diverse groups – with things like family policies and normalising flexible working – it enables everyone to enjoy the benefits. There is no downside for men when we improve things for women.

We have dismissed the fact that construction can't do flexible working on site, as companies have tested and trialled it and shown that it is possible without losing productivity. It's time the industry started thinking differently not only to bring women in but to retain those who are already here.

The biggest thing for potential male allies is awareness, which you will now have having read the various experiences of real women and what they face throughout this book. You will inevitably see things you may not have done before.

There are role models and allies both in and outside of the industry we can all learn from. Connect with them, learn from them, follow them on social media, work with them and use their advice to help you on your own allyship journey.

Most of all we have demonstrated that women know mistakes will be made and we are totally OK with that! Do not let fear of making a mistake stop you. Allyship is not always straightforward and can be a tough and uncomfortable journey, but the most important thing is that you start the journey.

NINE
What Can We Do To Make Things Better?

The construction industry is amazing and creative, but it is a people industry and it's an industry that's suffering from a huge skills shortage and an aging workforce. It also has a lack of diversity, particularly in gender, along with a huge leaky pipeline when it comes to retaining women long term in the industry.

When I started writing this book, I was on a mission to improve things for women in the industry, having realised many were facing the same issues I had when I started my career thirty years ago. I was and still am convinced that women do not need 'fixing' just because we work in a predominantly male environment.

It is clear many within the industry do not realise the issues women face so this book should raise awareness of them so that we can improve the culture and help plug the leak.

However, we have also seen it's not just a 'construction industry' problem and we have looked at the research that shows the issues women face globally in all countries and industries and how these are sometimes compounded in industries like construction.

We have investigated the specific issues troubling women in construction and seen the quite frankly horrifying statistics the results of my survey have shown. Women and role models in and outside the industry have provided advice to help women navigate some of the issues they face.

However, it isn't just about women. We lose two men every working day to suicide in UK construction so what is really needed is wholesale culture change.

We have seen that some countries and companies are better at creating inclusive cultures and that better diversity leads directly to happier teams and higher profitability but how do we make wholesale culture change? After all, lots of companies and institutions are trying to create change but the pace is glacial. It's not just about policies, key performance indicators (KPIs) or role models; much of it is about understanding the issues and then working to be allies to help create change every single day, calling out the bad behaviours and helping others to learn and grow – so that microaggressions, discrimination against women, outright sexism, and assault and bullying become the rarity rather than the norm that they currently are.

So what can we do?

Create inclusive cultures and behaviours starting with leadership

Everyone has a story, and once we listen to them we can better understand how others are affected. This book has provided numerous facts and figures and real life lived experiences of women in the industry that show we have a toxic culture in much of the industry that isn't inclusive and this needs to be acknowledged and dealt with.

When it comes to inclusivity, even the most privileged of us will have been excluded from something in life. It may be the football or netball team at school or the event at work, but if people take a moment to remember that feeling and recall the discomfort of feeling excluded, they can relate to how many women are feeling daily.

But relating to that feeling isn't all that's needed. For culture to change it has to start from the top. Everyone needs to work together and industry leaders need to model the right behaviours and ensure all teams are educated and that we are disseminating that culture down to all levels in organisations and throughout all partners and workers in the industry.

We need to remove the barriers for women and stop expecting women to mould themselves into something they aren't to cope with the often-hostile workplaces and environments they currently experience. Leaders of institutions and organisations need to put in place systems that not only challenge but abolish the behaviours that drive women out of the industry, and we need to ensure men become actively involved in gender diversity; this is proven to affect progress positively, with 96% of companies where men are actively involved reporting progress versus only 30% where men are not involved.[242]

So what can we do to change the culture?

It starts from the top – but educate teams

The industry will not change without educating everyone. This does not mean just in the leadership team within an industry institution, Tier 1 contractor or consulting firm either.

Some Tier 1 firms are making huge strides to change culture but even the best leadership there won't make a difference if that culture isn't embedded throughout the industry, which is made up mostly of SMEs. Culture change has to flow down throughout ALL industry and include all supply chain partners right down to the sole trader who may be working on site.

We are a people industry so let's introduce KPIs and goals not just for productivity, commerciality and programme but also for culture and behaviours. Introduce bonus measures around diversity and culture to encourage change from everyone.

Let's use technology to introduce apps or websites or use independent employee assistance reporting plans where people can anonymously and safely report issues without fear of retaliation.

When it comes to sites, we need site inductions that include specific sections on culture and behaviour, and we need to ensure the right behaviours are rewarded and the wrong ones are properly dealt with.

Stop forcing women into NDAs and compromise agreements

If we say we want more women in the industry our actions have to match it and currently they don't.

Companies say they want diversity and they want women and preach about having zero tolerance of inappropriate behaviour towards women yet it is obvious from my research that this is often not the case.

In the last three and a half years I have spoken to *ninety-eight women* who have been silenced by NDAs or compromise agreements after speaking out. We only have to look at Pregnant Then Screwed research to see these numbers are far worse for working mothers.

We must stop silencing women and paying them to go quietly when they report bullying or sexual harassment or when they have children or need more flexibility.

We need to stop protecting the perpetrators and keeping them in place because they are a 'good PM/

site manager who gets the job done' or a commercial manager that 'makes profit'.

The evidence is clear that more diversity leads to happier teams, more innovation and profit, so let's make it more welcoming for women and safe for them to stay and plug that proverbial leaky pipeline.

Inclusivity for women specifically

We need to make the industry inclusive from the word go – women need PPE that fits them, they need toilets that are clean and available when they need them, and they need facilities like breastfeeding rooms if they are mothers etc.

It should not have taken thirty years to get the PPE Revolution Campaign and #PPEthatfits campaigns off the ground.

There is some great kit out there for women, but we need to stop procurement from always picking the cheapest or bulk buy option and remember the 'personal' in PPE must be appropriate for the user – all users.

PPE is not a 'nice to have'; it is a requirement, and it must be suitable for the person wearing it, so provide it and don't moan that a women's jacket is more expensive and try to force them into PPE that does not fit to save a few pounds!

Manufacturers need to work with industry so that women's PPE is seen and so that what's available reaches all parts of the supply chain, right down to the sole trader on site.

These things are not big in the scheme of things, but the industry must change its attitudes toward procurement and site set-up, particularly if we want more women to stay in the industry post motherhood and menopause in site or trade roles.

If we are to make things in the industry better for women we need this to be led from the top of all organisations. We need leadership who want progress on gender parity and are willing to communicate this and be actively involved in increasing representation of women and having zero tolerance to inappropriate behaviour.

Stop trying to fix women – offer development and mentoring programmes to men and women together

As we have seen, women do not need fixing. In fact many of the issues women face with confidence are as a direct result of their surroundings and the years of discrimination in the workplace they have faced, including bias and often daily microaggressions.

Removing barriers such as those who bully and harass women is a great start, but then we need to look at what we can do to develop *everyone* in the workplace. Developing people is how the culture will change.

One thing we can do is to stop singling women out for different types of development and leadership training because they need 'more confidence'. While some gender-specific training can be productive there are disadvantages to separating genders, including amplifying gender stereotypes (such as the idea that women need leadership training because they don't have the same naturally occurring leadership traits as men).

The industry is currently predominantly male and if we want industry to become more inclusive and diverse, we need to develop people together. This enables people to learn and appreciate the issues others face. For men, listening and learning from the women they work with can help them take that knowledge and work on how they can make the workplace more equitable.

Sharing programmes can help create more inclusive leaders with better emotional and gender intelligence.

It's the same principle I often say in respect of 'women's conferences' – they are great, but women know what the issues are! What we need is to have men in the room to listen and learn about the experiences women have and then work with us to create a better culture for all of us.

The issues in the industry are not just a women's problem; they are an 'us' problem. Therefore, when it comes to development we can also consider putting men through specific allyship programmes, workshops, and coaching where they are encouraged to expand their views by hearing different views from co-workers with anonymised 360 questionnaires and challenged to stretch their communication skills and self-awareness.

Companies can introduce mentoring programmes that specifically include reverse mentoring, ensuring diversity across gender, age and other characteristics. This provides knowledge and access to people many women may not otherwise have and is a great way of educating those in managerial and leadership roles on the issues others face. Mentoring relationships with men who are willing to not only mentor but also go beyond that role and sponsor and use their influence to advocate for women and other diverse groups is fundamental.

To change the culture we need to invest in training for all employees and celebrate the wins. We already know that women in the industry feel DEI programmes can alienate men, so we need to work to ensure that changes.

Change the language

It's time to stop referring to construction as a 'male-dominated industry'. I admit I have used those words myself in the past when describing the industry. I have spoken in schools and colleges, at conferences and in podcasts and interviews and used this very phrase.

So what was it that altered my view?

The use of this terminology was raised by a woman in the audience at a conference a couple of years ago and it got me thinking about the language we use.

The Cambridge Dictionary describes the word 'dominate' as: 'to have control over a place or person'.[243]

As a woman entering the construction industry at the age of 18, I certainly didn't join the industry because I wanted to be 'dominated by' or 'controlled by' men and I certainly don't want to be now.

Therefore it seems to me that using the phrase 'male-dominated' to describe the industry in the twenty-first century is wrong. After all, if we continue to perpetuate language that puts men in a position of dominance over women, we will never resolve the issues and achieve equality.

Therefore, my first ask for anyone reading this book is that you go out there and start changing the language you use. Stop saying it's a male-dominated industry and start saying it has traditionally been 'predominantly male' but this is changing.

Let's stop giving young people, particularly young women, the impression this is an industry full of men where they will not only be in the minority but, due to the language, will potentially be dominated by men.

That is not the only language we can change. While I love construction it does have a reputation for being dirty and dangerous and I am sure we have all often said or heard of the 'hairy-arsed builders' that work in it.

Is the word 'construction' itself due for a revamp?

While it's true the industry can be dirty and certainly dangerous in places and, yes, sometimes there may even be hairy-arsed men working on building sites, do we want to continue 'not selling' the industry that way?

Perhaps a more inclusive term is in order which embraces all of the diversities of construction (ie including the multitude of varied roles that are available across the industry, not just based on or around a building site or the 'construction' itself).

I spoke to a prominent industry professional who chose to remain anonymous and she said:

> 'Instead of saying construction industry, which brings connotations of dirty building sites and builders all being men, why not change the language to "The Built Environment"? Just that change alone makes the industry more inclusive and can help remove some of the perceptions people have.'

So what if we start selling the industry as the diverse industry it is by referring to it as 'the built environment' rather than only using the word 'construction'.

Listen, educate and sell STEM

We have seen research shows just how young children are when they start to develop gender biases as a result of social constructs and the environment they are in and that even when we try to ensure they do not develop these biases we cannot control what they see outside the home. Remember Ceri's daughter in Chapter 7? Even with a mum doing everything possible to promote women in the industry children are still shaped into gendered behaviour by external influences.

For children that don't have a mum like Ceri this could mean they not only think in a gendered way but start to dismiss studying STEM subjects, as well as dismissing the various career opportunities in the built environment.

We need to work harder to ensure children are not forced into narrow ways of thinking and some of this means getting in to see them when they are really young in primary education, well before that age of six where the gender stereotypes have set in.

We need to work with education itself as I have realised over the years that teachers, lecturers and even career advisors are often unaware of the various careers on offer, even in secondary schools and in higher education. They also do not know the many different pathways that there are to get into the industry. Not every child wants to study their way into a career and there are so many apprenticeship opportunities across the board in the industry where people can work and study at the same time or learn a trade. We need to make this clearer.

We need to educate children and teachers and it's why some of the work STEMAZING and STEM

WHAT CAN WE DO TO MAKE THINGS BETTER?

Ambassadors do, particularly in younger education settings, is so good.

We all need to be targeting the youngest generations, so we stop the stereotyping from starting.

Offer flexible working to allow work-life balance for everyone

While this book is about women in the industry it is also a fact that I want to make things better for men as well. We know that more women in leadership and more diverse teams create happier teams, better innovation and profit but we have to make things better for everyone, not just for women.

For parents, while women are the ones who give birth, we must remove the assumption that they will always be the primary carer. We need to close the motherhood gap and work to prevent the fatherhood forfeit and work on attitudes that men and some women have when men decide to take paternity leave or share maternity leave with their partners. We need to ensure all parents have the choice to spend time with their children.

We aren't living in the 1950s anymore where women stayed at home and men went to work. Most families now have both parents working; therefore all parents need to have the opportunity to be actively involved in their children's lives. Men should not be experiencing pressure from societal expectations that they should only be the 'breadwinner' or 'provider'; they should be given the opportunity to be as involved in their children's lives as they want. This means offering flexibility to all.

Those companies that offer paid leave beyond the abysmal statutory leave the UK Government offers are setting a great example, as are people like Elliot Rae with his #ParentingOutLoud campaign encouraging men to shout about their caring responsibilities at work and normalise dads' caregiving.[244]

But it's more than just looking after children; we have an aging population and with that often comes additional caring responsibilities. We need to think of everyone and there are some really easy ways to ensure we are being more inclusive, such as thinking of parents and carers:

- ⚲ Start meetings later and finish earlier to allow child pick up/caring responsibilities.

- ⚲ For team days or events, consider setting them at different times or providing childcare facilities so parents can attend. Stop making people miss out if they are parents or have caring responsibilities.

- ⚲ Be flexible.

New ways of working in construction

We all know about modular building and the difference that can make to quality and manpower requirements as well as speed of construction, but it is equally as important to look at new ways of working, particularly on site.

I spoke to Lee Marley, CEO at Lee Marley Brickwork (LMB), as one of the things that I wanted to cover is how women can potentially assist in helping bridge the trades skills gap in the industry. We discussed some of the solutions.

LMB has a graduate programme and regularly has women going through this, training to be professional bricklayers. One of the things Lee instigated to try and solve some of the issues with recruitment and retention of bricklayers is the opening of LMB's own college for people of all genders, which opened in September 2023. This was predominantly because Lee felt apprentices were not getting adequate training from the various colleges in the UK. This innovative move ensures the thirty-six apprentices a year they will take on will be fully trained in modern methods of construction and be 'work ready', setting participants up for life with excellent skills for a lucrative career in the industry.

We spoke about some of the other things the industry could do using different solutions.

The working day

Currently working systems in the UK on building sites are non-flexible. They expect work to be done five days a week and sometimes on a Saturday, which often means a different pay structure and no flexibility for companies or their staff, particularly as a large proportion of the UK construction industry is made up of SMEs.

This in turn means the industry isn't inclusive and this particularly affects those with caring responsibilities as there is little flexibility for caring arrangements.

Using bricklaying as an example, bricklayers can work at a laying rate rather than a day rate. If they worked on productivity it wouldn't matter about the hours. In fact a gang working well could get everything done in four or five hours rather than all day, which would enable them to have the flexibility to work around childcare or care arrangements for example.

When looking at factory brickwork production there are hourly rates for a gang and this seems totally feasible for sites in the UK.

If we look at Dubai as an example, they often work on a four-days-on, three-days-off scenario; this is another method the industry could try. Using methods like these would lead to reduced issues with overtime costs and enable people to arrange childcare or other care requirements around shifts.

Job shares

Job shares and flexi working would also work brilliantly if the emphasis was on productivity rather than just having bodies on site.

One prominent woman I spoke to in more depth, with specific reference to site roles and how the industry could improve, was Katie Kelleher, former crane operator but now the Construction Plant-hire Association's Technical and Development Officer.

Katie entered construction following a career change and was the first woman on the Lifting Technician apprenticeship with Select/Laing O'Rourke becoming a crane operator on projects like Crossrail and Thames Tideway. Katie loves cranes and all and she is passionate about her STEM work and showcasing construction careers but the big question I had to ask her was why the change?

Sadly the answer I got did not surprise me and is one that other women in the industry have also given: the lack of flexibility.

Crane drivers are often expected to be on site at 7am–7.30am and will often be there until 6pm (or later if a delivery is late). Then there are weekends where operators may be expected to be there on a Saturday. This, mixed with the increasing pushes for a shorter lunch break so more lifts can be done, is not conducive to family life or those with other commitments. As Katie said, 'The industry is not all about projects, it has to start with people. Companies and sites need to understand their people and, more importantly, care about them. The next generation do not want to work the way we have in the past.'

So how can we improve things for the future? One idea for skills such as crane and plant operators is to have a split shift system similar to the job share scenario you may see in industries such as banking or insurance or the NHS and companies like Network Rail and TfL.

Could this work in construction and enable us not only to attract but to keep diverse and skilled talent? The answer appears to be yes. For example, if two highly skilled operators who cannot work ten- to twelve-hour days, due to other commitments, could share the role, this would avoid problems, such as:

- The crane operator would be there for the time needed for the project, keeping the project on schedule.
- It would enable operators to arrange care commitments around their working pattern

with no stress that they would be late home and unable for example to collect children from childcare. Both would know their shift hours and these would not change unless by prior agreement. This provides security not only for the operators but also the contractor on the project who has a programme to keep to.

- Safety would be improved for the operators. Traditionally crane operators work long hours and often stay in the confined cab of the crane for long periods (sometimes all day). The risks of operator fatigue would be eliminated.[245]

- Health issues commonly seen in crane operators would be reduced. Sitting in a cab all day poses greater risks of musculoskeletal disorders,[246] poor circulation, headaches and other health conditions that become prevalent in stationary type roles.[247]

Improved childcare/clubs/vouchers

If we look at companies like Next and BP, they offer subsidised nurseries and childcare vouchers. Can the industry emulate this?

Some companies do offer vouchers and support. What if, in cities like London where lots of construction projects are happening, construction companies clubbed together to provide a number of subsidised childcare facilities around the city that staff from the different companies could use?

This could work well, and it would enable costs to be shared/reduced while allowing parents of different companies the opportunity to work/come back to work sooner. It could also be something that adds another income stream for the companies that try it.

As with all ideas, the problem is often that it takes someone being innovative enough to introduce these ideas. It's clear the industry could easily do flexi working, rolling shifts or four-day weeks where just as much productivity was achieved, but it needs someone to start that process and show it works to encourage others to do the same... rather like the contractors that trialled flexi working earlier in the book. Who is brave enough to trial these ideas and make real cultural change for the future?

What can you do?

We all have the potential to make an impact and help change the industry (and everywhere in our lives come to think of it!). Let's think about the things we can *all* do regardless of our age, gender, race, sexuality, religion or any other difference/s we may have.

This list is not exhaustive, but I hope it gives anyone reading this some simple things you can start doing immediately when you put the book down.

WHAT CAN WE DO TO MAKE THINGS BETTER?

Remember what equity means

It means each person has what they need to perform, and this will be different for every person. Some may need a number of accommodations to enable them to have the same opportunities as others, and that's OK. I love this picture that is licensed for free use by everyone as it perfectly explains the difference between equality and equity as we do not all need the same things! But what about if we worked together to get rid of the fence... surely that's what we should be aiming for?

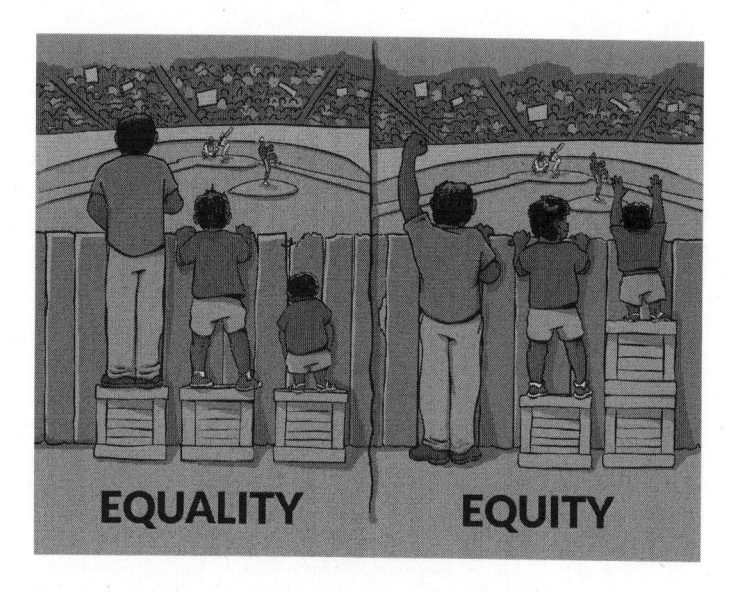

Illustrating equality vs equity (Interaction Institute for Social Change | Artist: Angus Maguire)

Share the book

OK, that may sound selfish as obviously I want people to read it, but the fact is some people may not think it's a book for them. I hope by now it's clear that while I want to improve things for women in the construction industry, I actually want to improve things for *everyone*. Part of that is in education. Share the book, talk about the statistics and case studies you have read. Even if you don't personally agree with everything in this book, now is the time to start those conversations and help people get on the journey to improving the culture in the industry.

People don't know what they don't know – you didn't know the statistics and issues women were having so now it's time to help others by sharing!

Be curious

I started saying this a long time ago and I have said it at various events. I've said it in keynote speeches, when I closed the IWD RICS conference in 2024, and when I chaired the *Construction News* and *New Civil Engineer*'s Inspiring Women in Construction Conference 2024.

It's a catchy phrase – 'be curious' – and one that I know many use. While it may not seem like an action per se, having a curious mind means you will be open and eager to learning something new. Part of the journey towards making things better is being curious and learning about the issues.

The fact is this book and my research are really a drop in the ocean of the issues we have but if you go out and do one thing new today, let it be to go out with an open mind so you can learn more, ask questions and share your knowledge with others.

Learn about your own bias

I've spoken about the biases we all have in this book, so learn about them; consider the subconscious ones you may not be aware of yourself. Undertake the Harvard Implicit Bias Test or watch Heineken's advert from 2017 that shows how people's bias can be overcome when we stop judging and instead take the time to listen and be open.[248] If we start to think about our own biases, we can challenge them and work on changing them and educating ourselves so that we can be better people moving forward.

If you work commercially in the industry – keep the payments moving

While this may not be considered to be something everyone can do, there will be many reading this who have responsibility for payments to various contractors, suppliers, consultants and subcontractors for works in construction. Whether as a surveyor on site, a subcontractor to a supplier or a small construction business to a self-employed tradesperson we need to keep the money flowing.

In 2023 there were about 882,770 SMEs in the construction sector in the UK.[249] These SMEs, and self-employed people contracted by them, are often the ones who suffer most when payments are delayed or valuations slashed. We all have bills to pay. There was a period in my childhood when my dad's business was hit hard by a builder not paying and it impacted our family hugely. The worry of my parents who may have lost the house while trying to clothe and feed three children was something I will never forget.

Think of the impacts you have on not just companies but on people and their families when you make these decisions. We are a people industry. Don't do things to others because someone up the line has slashed your valuation. That is not right or fair.

Many SMEs and self-employed people do not have budgets and emergency funds to cope, and it can have huge impacts on mental health when people are worrying about becoming homeless or being able to pay the bills and eat.

We lose two men every working day in construction and need to do everything we can to prevent additional stress in an often already stressful environment.

Put yourself in the other's shoes

As you have seen from reading this book and all the research that has gone into it, people in construction are suffering. You as a reader may be OK but many in the industry are not.

Women are being bullied, sexually harassed, violated, held back in their careers and in many cases silenced by companies who preach their concern for women but then continue to regularly put women on NDAs and compromise agreements to stop them from speaking out rather than treating them with respect and dignity.

We have a mental health crisis with men in the industry who are suffering and an alarming suicide rate.

It's so easy to rush around in our daily lives, particularly when under pressure with deadlines. We may snap at people or dismiss them when they want to talk or, worse, ignore them or in the name of banter say something as a 'joke' that could genuinely cause them harm.

We all need to stop and take a moment to consider what someone else may have going on.

Consider different ways of working when you have children

Use the Wilders from Chapter 8 as an example. Discuss how you will make childcare work for both parties in a relationship and tackle it together so you come to a position that works for you, whether that's four-day weeks, nine-day fortnights or a different option altogether. Follow Elliot Rae, founder of 'Parenting Out Loud', and support his campaign to change workplace culture and encourage working dads to be proud of caring responsibilities.

Follow/connect with others

Please also remember these are not the only women doing great things. For example, I wrote about Katherine Evans and her work around PPE in Chapter 3, and the final section in Chapter 8 has further suggestions of individuals, organisations and networks to follow or connect with. But this section gives direct advice from women working hard to make things better, so do take on board what they say here, seek them out, connect on LinkedIn and work together so everyone in construction can win.

Chai and Chat Engineering Podcast

Set up by three South Asian engineers – Dipalee Jukes, Era Shah and Malika Kapasi – who felt like outliers in their professions because they couldn't see other people like them at work, this podcast highlights and brings awareness to other amazing women engineers.

https://open.spotify.com/show/7D5CxK71d0YoDgZ6IofeEb

Engineering Rebuilt Podcast

Yvonne Raleigh, Tina Gunnarsson and Lina Soderberg interview people to shine a light on women in the construction industry.

https://podcasts.apple.com/us/podcast/engineering-rebuilt/id1626146764

#YesSheCan

While not limited to construction, this organisation aims to inspire women to take the next step and put themselves forward. Its mantra is 'she believes, so she leads' and I have taken part in a podcast with them.

www.yes-shecan.com

Skills 4

Founded by Jayne Little, Skills 4 benefits from first-hand experience in the challenges of STEM. It offers award-winning training to help attract, retain and progress diverse talent, and it has a great set of podcasts.

https://skills4training.org

Catching Bees

LinkedIn and Instagram accounts run by Lisa Martello, a construction project manager with experience of working in Australia and the UK. Lisa is passionate about equality and shares amazing perspectives in her Catching Bees posts.

www.linkedin.com/company/catching-bees

Bold as Brass

LinkedIn group run by Katherine Evans (as mentioned in Chapters 3 and 5).

www.linkedin.com/groups/12683758

Women In Construction Hub

Michaela Wain created this hub for women in construction to connect. If you connect with her on LinkedIn, she will send you a link to the various 'Hub' groups on WhatsApp.

www.linkedin.com/in/michaela-wain-8860284a

Lee Chambers

Available to follow on LinkedIn, Lee posts every day and offers brilliant keynote speeches and allyship programmes that can make a real difference.

www.linkedin.com/in/leechambers-1

Jo Phillips

Available to follow on LinkedIn, Jo is a coach and the MD/founder of The Woman Behind the Women (https://thewomanbehindthewomen.com/jo-phillips). Her Level Up Programme works with employee resource groups to help retain women in the pipeline, by showing women how to handle microaggressions and how to map their own ideas. She also runs allyship programmes and mentoring programmes. She often provides free sessions to ensure as many women as possible can benefit.

www.linkedin.com/in/jo-p-thewomanbehind thewomen

Summary

This chapter has been about what we can all do to make the culture better. This ranges from institutions and companies taking different approaches to culture, leadership and training of staff to considering the use of our language in the everyday that may inadvertently 'put people off'.

We all need to work on our biases both at work and at home and we need to ensure the next generations do not become gender biased by the age of six. We need to embrace those young minds and nurture them so that we don't have girls thinking they can't to maths or science and that trades roles are only for boys.

We must continue to get into primary education as well as later education and show children the opportunities the industry has to offer. Things are changing and with the introduction of AI the future of the industry will be very different, so let's get young minds interested now so they can help create better ways of doing things.

Yes, I know there are some dinosaurs in the industry that we will never be able to change, but if enough people start changing these dinosaurs will no longer have a place.

It's time to make the bullies, harassers and worse extinct from the industry. This means everyone needs to stop hiding bad behaviours and covering them up for the sake of profit or keeping things quiet and we need to stop paying women off.

If we all do things, we will create a ripple that grows and helps improve things for those around us and in the wider industry. Join me and make the change!

Conclusion

The industry and wider built environment is great but at the moment it is an industry that is sick. We have skills shortages and a toxic culture in many places, terrible mental health and suicide statistics for men and an epically large leak in the pipeline for the few women who do enter the industry.

For women who manage to stay, they are battle-beaten and exhausted after years of fighting. Women have been watching men consistently be promoted over them, be paid more than them, steal ideas from them, speak over them and generally in many places be treated better than them.

We have looked at global issues in the workplace, the gender pay gap, the motherhood penalty and the fatherhood forfeit, and we have looked specifically at global issues around sexual harassment.

We have also looked at why diversity in gender (and full stop) is better for everyone. We have seen evidence of happier teams, increased profits and better innovation – diversity is good for all.

However, we have also looked specifically at how the industry treats women. We've seen the horrifying figures around the bullying and harassment of women, and statistics that showed 30% of women I surveyed had experienced sexual assault in the workplace in their career and that 16 sexual assaults had happened in the year 2022–2023.

We have a situation where 62% of women have been bullied and of those who reported it a large percentage were made to feel they were too sensitive or emotional rather than the issues being taken seriously.

We wonder why we have a leak and can't get more than 12–15% of women in the industry and even less than 2% in trades.

For the women reading this I hope you have a feeling of relief that finally someone has stood up and spoken loudly about what is happening. This is not hidden anymore. The statistics are out there and many of your experiences have been shared and, as horrifying as some of them are, thank you for trusting me with them.

I hear you and I see you and I will continue to fight for you to have a better workplace and for all the future generations not to have to deal with the pain and suffering many of us have.

CONCLUSION

For women who haven't experienced the issues covered, I hope you have some understanding of why so many women do leave and will help me to ensure others have your experience instead.

For the men who have read this – thank you. It won't have been easy, but I hope you see that I also want things to be better for you too. We cannot keep losing men to suicide. For you the mission is perhaps more difficult. You have now read the issues women face and we have looked at the patriarchy and how it's as damaging for most men as it is for women. We have looked at things you may not have considered before, in respect of everyday bias and behaviours, but now that you know these things I hope you will notice them.

Next time a woman is spoken over or ignored, I hope you not only see it but take the advice of the various role models and play your part in shaping a better future by calling it out.

We need your allyship, but please remember it's an active role and most of all remember it's OK to make mistakes; women know that will happen and we are here to work with you.

The time has come to join me and make the change.

Notes

1. ONS, 'Dataset: EMP13: Employment by industry' (13 February 2025), www.ons.gov.uk/employmentandlabourmarket/peopleinwork/employmentandemployeetypes/datasets/employmentbyindustryemp13, accessed 23 February 2025. Please refer to Appendix 1 on my website buildingwomen.co.uk, which takes the ONS data and provides the yearly percentages in a table.
2. Chartered Institute of Building, 'Future of construction: Equality, diversity and inclusion', www.ciob.org/industry/policy-research/policy-positions/equality-diversity-inclusion, accessed 2 March 2025
3. D Clark, 'Gross value added of the construction sector in the United Kingdom from 1990 to 2023', *Statista* (11 September 2024), www.statista.com/statistics/760094/construction-sector-gross-value-added-in-the-uk/#statisticContainer, accessed 17 January 2025

4. ONS, 'Dataset: EMP13: Employment by industry' (13 February 2025), www.ons.gov.uk/employmentandlabourmarket/peopleinwork/employmentandemployeetypes/datasets/employmentbyindustryemp13, accessed 23 February 2025. Please refer to Appendix 1 on my website buildingwomen.co.uk, which takes the ONS data and provides the detailed breakdown at the tab 'ONS Averages Table'.
5. Chartered Institute of Building, 'Future of construction: Equality, diversity and inclusion', www.ciob.org/industry/policy-research/policy-positions/equality-diversity-inclusion, accessed 2 March 2025
6. M Latham, *Constructing the Team: Joint review of procurement and contractual arrangements in the United Kingdom construction industry* (HMSO, 1994), https://constructingexcellence.org.uk/wp-content/uploads/2014/10/Constructing-the-team-The-Latham-Report.pdf, paragraph 7.24
7. CIOB, *Diversity and Inclusion in Construction*, Special Report (2021) p4, www.ciob.org/media/1181/download, accessed 2 June 2023; www.ciob.org/specialreport/charter/diversityandinclusion, accessed 2 June 2023
8. UN Department of Economic and Social Affairs, 'Goals', https://sdgs.un.org/goals/goal5, accessed 5 September 2023
9. UN Regional Information Centre, 'Women and girls: Brilliant minds in technology', https://unric.org/en/women-and-girls-brilliant-minds-in-technology, accessed 15 April 2023
10. C Fine, *Delusions of Gender* (Icon Books, 2005)
11. L Bian et al, 'Gender stereotypes about intellectual ability emerge early and influence children's interests', *Science*, 355 (2017), 389–391, www.science.org/doi/10.1126/science.aah6524, accessed 5 September 2023
12. Fawcett Society, *Unlimited Potential: Report of the Commission on Gender Stereotypes in Early Childhood* (2020), www.fawcettsociety.org.uk/Handlers/Download.ashx?IDMF=17fb0c11-f904-469c-a62e-173583d441c8, accessed 5 September 2023

NOTES

13. D Reilly, D Nuemann and G Andrews, 'Gender differences in self-estimated intelligence: Exploring the male hubris, female humility problem', *Frontiers*, 13 (2022), www.frontiersin.org/journals/psychology/articles/10.3389/fpsyg.2022.812483/full, accessed 6 March 2025
14. B Henebery, 'Are girls smarter than boys? Here's what the science says', *The Educator* (14 October 2021), www.theeducatoronline.com/k12/news/are-girls-smarter-than-boys-heres-what-the-science-says/278940, accessed 6 March 2025; D Giofrè et al, 'Sex/gender differences in general cognitive abilities: An investigation using the Leiter-3', *Cogn Process*, 25 (2024), 663–672, https://pmc.ncbi.nlm.nih.gov/articles/PMC11541283, accessed 6 March 2025; L Clarence-Smith, 'Trend of underperforming boys ignored "because of focus on girl's achievement"', *The Telegraph* (21 August 2023), www.telegraph.co.uk/news/2023/08/21/school-underperforming-boys-ignored-focus-on-girls, accessed 6 March 2025
15. Education and Employers, 'Redraw the balance' (2016), www.educationandemployers.org/17497-2, accessed 6 March 2025
16. Engineering UK, 'Diversity challenges in engineering and technology', www.engineeringuk.com/research-and-insights/industry-and-workforce/diversity-challenges-in-engineering-and-technology, accessed 9 February 2025. Women made up just 16.5% of the engineering workforce in 2022 and this dropped to 15.7% in 2023, with gender disparity seen throughout all educational pathways into engineering.
17. NBS, 'Construction now an "attractive" career path for 50% of young adults' (10 August 2022), www.thenbs.com/about-nbs/press-releases/construction-now-an-attractive-career-path-for-50-of-young-adults, accessed 5 September 2023
18. The Smith Institute, *Building the Future: Women in construction* (2014), https://smithinstitutethinktank.wordpress.com/wp-content/uploads/2014/09/building-the-future-women-in-construction.pdf, accessed 6 March 2025

19 Institution of Mechanical Engineers, *Stay or Go: The experience of female engineers in early career* (2017), www.imeche.org/policy-and-press/reports/detail/stay-or-go.-the-experience-of-female-engineers-in-early-career, accessed 11 April 2023
20 D Barnes, *CIOB Response to the APPG for Excellence in the Built Environment Inquiry into the Recruitment and Retention of More Women into the Construction Sector* (2019), www.ciob.org/media/124/download, accessed 9 February 2025
21 RICS global database of circa 139,000 members, February 2022 (provided to me by Sybil Taunton, Head of Diversity, Equity and Inclusion, RICS)
22 RICS, *Women in Surveying: Insight report* (2023), www.rics.org/news-insights/rics-launches-its-first-women-in-surveying-insight-report, accessed 9 February 2025
23 L Ellison and E Cowling, *Raising the Ratio Research: What motivates women to leave the profession* (Kingston University, 2006)
24 RICS, *Women in Surveying* (2023), p12, figure 12
25 Engineering UK, *Women in Engineering and Technology* (2024), www.engineeringuk.com/media/bryloncz/women-in-engineering-2024-update-engineeringuk-may-2024.pdf, accessed 9 July 2024
26 BBC News, 'Jacinda Ardern to quit: "I no longer have enough in the tank"' (19 January 2023), www.bbc.co.uk/news/av/world-asia-64327453, accessed 13 March 2025
27 I Brownlie, 'Sturgeon steps down: I'm a human being – I have regrets, says Nicola Sturgeon', *The Scottish Sun* (15 February 2023), www.thescottishsun.co.uk/news/10226156/im-human-being-i-have-regrets-says-nicola-sturgeon, accessed 13 March 2025
28 S Wojcicki, 'A personal update from Susan', *Inside YouTube* (16 February 2023), https://blog.youtube/inside-youtube/a-personal-update-from-susan, accessed 13 March 2025
29 McKinsey & Company and LeanIn.Org, *Women in the Workplace 2024*, www.mckinsey.com/featured-insights/diversity-and-inclusion/women-in-the-workplace,

accessed 7 September 2023; *Women in the Workplace 2023*, www.mckinsey.com/featured-insights/diversity-and-inclusion/women-in-the-workplace-2023, accessed 9 February 2025; *Women in the Workplace 2022*, www.mckinsey.com/featured-insights/diversity-and-inclusion/women-in-the-workplace-archive, accessed 9 February 2025

30 McKinsey & Company and Leanin.Org, *Women in the Workplace 2022*, www.mckinsey.com/featured-insights/diversity-and-inclusion/women-in-the-workplace-archive, accessed 9 February 2025

31 Ibid

32 K Mangino, *Equal Partners: Improving gender equality at home* (St Martin's Press, 2022)

33 T Warren and C Lyonette, 'Carrying the work burden of the Covid-19 pandemic: Working class women in the UK, Briefing Note 2: Housework and childcare'. Working Paper No 2020/2 (Nottingham University Business School, December 2020), www.nottingham.ac.uk/business/documents/research/carrying-the-work-burden-of-covid-19/briefing-note-2.pdf, accessed 29 October 2023

34 ONS, 'Parenting in lockdown: Coronavirus and the effects on work-life balance' (2020), www.ons.gov.uk/peoplepopulationandcommunity/healthandsocialcare/conditionsanddiseases/articles/parentinginlockdowncoronavirusandtheeffectsonworklifebalance/2020-07-22, accessed 29 October 2023

35 National Centre for Social Research, *British Social Attitudes 2023*, https://natcen.ac.uk/events/british-social-attitudes-2023, accessed 29 October 2024

36 Employee Benefits, 'Father awarded £20,000 after gossip about his flexible working' (25 October 2024), https://employeebenefits.co.uk/employee-engagement/father-awarded-20000-after-gossip-about-his-flexible-working/279908.article, accessed 25 October 2024

37 E Filby, 'Why Gen Z daughters won't follow in their mums' career footsteps', *City AM* (24 October 2023),

www.cityam.com/why-gen-z-daughters-wont-follow-in-their-mums-career-footsteps, accessed 28 October 2023

38 World Health Organization, 'Improving women's health and gender justice since the 1995 Beijing Platform for Action' (2021), www.who.int/initiatives/beijing25, accessed 9 February 2025

39 World Economic Forum, *Global Gender Gap Report 2022*, www3.weforum.org/docs/WEF_GGGR_2022.pdf, accessed 11 July 2024

40 World Economic Forum, *Global Gender Gap Report 2023*, www3.weforum.org/docs/WEF_GGGR_2023.pdf, accessed 11 July 2024

41 World Economic Forum, *Global Gender Gap Report 2024*, www3.weforum.org/docs/WEF_GGGR_2024.pdf, accessed 11 July 2024

42 UN News, 'Report reveals nearly 90 per cent of all people have "a deeply ingrained bias" against women' (5 March 2020), https://news.un.org/en/story/2020/03/1058731, accessed 21 January 2023; UNDP, *2020 Gender Social Norms Index (GSNI): Tackling Social Norms: A game changer for gender inequalities* (2020), https://hdr.undp.org/content/2020-gender-social-norms-index-gsni, accessed 9 February 2025

43 UNDP, 'Frequently asked questions', *Tackling Social Norms: A game changer for gender inequalities* (2020), https://hdr.undp.org/system/files/documents/frequentlyaskedquestionsgsni.pdf, accessed 11 July 2024

44 Shape Talent, *The Three Barriers Preventing Women from Progressing in Corporate UK Today* (2022), www.shapetalent.com/wp-content/uploads/2023/03/20230323-Gender-Equality-UK-Report-FINAL.pdf, accessed 14 September 2024

45 UN Women, *Progress on the Sustainable Development Goals: The gender snapshot 2022* (2022), www.unwomen.org/en/digital-library/publications/2022/09/progress-on-the-sustainable-development-goals-the-gender-snapshot-2022, accessed 27 March 2023

46 World Economic Forum, *Global Gender Gap Report 2022*, www3.weforum.org/docs/WEF_GGGR_2022.pdf, accessed 11 July 2024
47 UN News, 'New UN report reveals chronic bias against women over last decade' (12 June 2023), https://news.un.org/en/story/2023/06/1137532, accessed 7 March 2025
48 UN, *The Sustainable Development Goals Report 2024*, https://unstats.un.org/sdgs/report/2024/The-Sustainable-Development-Goals-Report-2024.pdf, accessed 11 July 2024, p20
49 UCSD Center On Gender Equity And Health and Stop Street Harassment, *Measuring #MeToo: A National Study on Sexual Harassment and Assault* (2019), https://stopstreetharassment.org/wp-content/uploads/2012/08/2019-MeToo-National-Sexual-Harassment-and-Assault-Report.pdf, accessed 22 December 2023
50 Statistics Canada, 'In 2020, one in four women and one in six men reported having experienced inappropriate sexualized behaviours at work in the previous year' (12 August 2021), www150.statcan.gc.ca/n1/daily-quotidien/210812/dq210812b-eng.htm, accessed 22 December 2023
51 Ibid
52 Australian Human Rights Commission, *Time for Respect: Fifth national survey sexual harassment workplaces* (2022), https://humanrights.gov.au/time-for-respect-2022, accessed 2 December 2023
53 Government Equalities Office, *2020 Sexual Harassment Survey*, https://assets.publishing.service.gov.uk/media/60f03e068fa8f50c77458285/2021-07-12_Sexual_Harassment_Report_FINAL.pdf, accessed 22 December 2023
54 Jamie Grierson, 'List of sexual misconduct allegations made against MPs', *The Guardian* (18 May 2022), www.theguardian.com/uk-news/2022/may/18/list-of-sexual-misconduct-allegations-made-against-mps, accessed 7 March 2025; L Neumeister, J Peltz and MR Sisak, 'Jury finds Trump liable for sexual

abuse, awards accuser $5M', *AP* (10 May 2023), https://apnews.com/article/trump-rape-carroll-trial-fe68259a4b98bb3947d42af9ec83d7db, accessed 7 March 2025; F Brown, 'Officials with diplomatic immunity accused of sexual assault and indecent exposure', *Sky News* (14 November 2024), https://news.sky.com/story/officials-with-diplomatic-immunity-accused-of-sexual-assault-and-indecent-exposure-13254290, accessed 7 March 2025

55 Sportanddev.org, 'Sexual harassment in sport' (10 December 2021), www.sportanddev.org/latest/news/sexual-harassment-sport, accessed 7 March 2025

56 Sky News, 'Luis Rubiales found guilty of sexual assault after kissing Jenni Hermoso without consent after World Cup final' (20 February 2025), https://news.sky.com/story/luis-rubiales-found-guilty-over-kissing-jenni-hermoso-after-womens-world-cup-final-13313194, accessed 7 March 2025

57 C Bennett, 'Hiring Nick Kyrgios to fill its vacant toxic male slot is an unforced error on BBC's part', *The Guardian* (25 May 2024), www.theguardian.com/commentisfree/article/2024/may/25/hiring-nick-kyrgios-to-fill-its-vacant-toxic-male-slot-is-an-unforced-error-on-bbcs-part, accessed 7 March 2025

58 ONS, 'Experiences of harassment in England and Wales: December 2023' (7 December 2023), www.ons.gov.uk/peoplepopulationandcommunity/crimeandjustice/bulletins/experiencesofharassmentinenglandandwales/december2023, accessed 18 July 2024

59 T Barta, M Kleiner and T Neumann, 'Is there a payoff from top-team diversity?', *McKinsey Quarterly* (1 April 2012), www.mckinsey.com/capabilities/people-and-organizational-performance/our-insights/is-there-a-payoff-from-top-team-diversity, accessed 15 May 2024

60 J Bourke, 'The diversity and inclusion revolution: Eight powerful truths', *Deloitte Review*, 22 (2018), www2.deloitte.com/us/en/insights/deloitte-review/issue-22/diversity-and-inclusion-at-work-eight-powerful-truths.html, accessed 10 July 2024

61 Deloitte's research also identified six signature traits for inclusive leaders – commitment, courage, cognizance of bias, curiosity, cultural intelligence and collaboration: J Bourke, 'The six signature traits of inclusive leadership', Deloitte (15 April 2016), www2.deloitte.com/us/en/insights/topics/talent/six-signature-traits-of-inclusive-leadership.html, accessed 10 July 2024

62 BCG, 'Inclusive advantage', www.bcg.com/publications/2019/winning-the-20s-business-imperative-of-diversity, accessed 11 July 2024

63 RJ Ely and DA Thomas, 'Getting serious about diversity: Enough already with the business case', *Harvard Business Review* (November–December 2020), https://hbr.org/2020/11/getting-serious-about-diversity-enough-already-with-the-business-case, accessed 11 July 2024

64 International Labour Organization, *Women in Business and Management: The business case for change* (2019), www.ilo.org/publications/women-business-and-management-business-case-change, accessed 15 September 2024

65 BoardReady, *Lessons from the Pandemic: Board diversity and performance* (2021), https://assets-global.website-files.com/61d633fd6b59246c2dc62e98/6271a21dc04d2e 13529daa84_BoardReady_Report_Final.pdf, accessed 11 July 2024

66 O Ozdemir et al, 'Corporate social responsibility and financial performance: Does board diversity matter?', *Journal of Global Business Insights*, 6/2 (2021), https://digitalcommons.usf.edu/globe/vol6/iss2/1, accessed 2 November 2024; E Varouchas et al, 'Board gender diversity and financial performance of US banks: Evidence from quantile regression', *Theoretical Economics Letters*, 13 (2023), 1737–1756, www.researchgate.net/publication/376852155_Board_Gender_Diversity_and_Financial_Performance_of_US_Banks_Evidence_from_Quantile_Regression, accessed 2 November 2024

67 O Ozdemir et al, 'Corporate social responsibility and financial performance: Does board diversity matter?',

Journal of Global Business Insights, 6/2 (2021), https://digitalcommons.usf.edu/globe/vol6/iss2/1, accessed 2 November 2024

68 B of A Securities, *Everybody Counts! Diversity and inclusion primer*, www.unilever.com/files/691af0c7-dc4d-4c8b-a23c-326a02b0a33b/everybody-counts-di-report.pdf, accessed 2 November 2024

69 Ibid

70 LN Simionescu et al, 'Does board gender diversity affect firm performance? Empirical evidence from Standard & Poor's 500 Information Technology Sector', *Financial Innovation*, 7/1 (2021), www.researchgate.net/publication/367868825_Does_board_gender_diversity_affect_firm_performance_Empirical_evidence_from_Standard_Poor's_500_Information_Technology_Sector, accessed 7 March 2025, p11

71 M Abebe and H Dadanlar, 'From tokens to key players: The influence of board gender and ethnic diversity on corporate discrimination lawsuits', *Human Relations*, 74/4 (2021), 527-555, https://doi.org/10.1177/0018726719888801, accessed 7 March 2025

72 V Hunt, D Layton and S Prince, 'Why diversity matters', *McKinsey & Company* (1 January 2015), www.mckinsey.com/capabilities/people-and-organizational-performance/our-insights/why-diversity-matters, accessed 2 November 2024; BCG, 'Inclusive advantage', www.bcg.com/publications/2021/building-an-inclusive-culture-leads-to-happier-healthier-workers, accessed 2 November 2024

73 M Hedayat, 'Diversity is not enough', *Forbes* (30 June 2020), www.forbes.com/sites/mursalhedayat/2020/06/30/diversity-is-not-enough, accessed 18 December 2024

74 McKinsey Global Institute, *The Power of Parity: How advancing women's equality can add $12 trillion to global growth* (2015), www.mckinsey.com/featured-insights/employment-and-growth/how-advancing-womens-equality-can-add-12-trillion-to-global-growth, accessed 11 July 2024

75 Universal Declaration of Human Rights, Article 1 and Article 2, www.un.org/sites/un2.un.org/files/2021/03/udhr.pdf, accessed 11 July 2024
76 UN, 'Sustainable Development Goals', www.un.org/sustainabledevelopment, accessed 11 July 2024
77 UN, 'Goal 5: Achieve gender equality and empower all women and girls', www.un.org/sustainabledevelopment/gender-equality, accessed 11 July 2024
78 Statistics Iceland, 'Unadjusted gender pay gap 9.1% in 2022' (17 August 2023), www.statice.is/publications/news-archive/wages-and-income/unadjusted-gender-pay-gap-2022, accessed 1 July 2024
79 LinkedIn, 'Gender equity in the workplace: Breaking down gender barriers and biases' (2022), https://linkedin.github.io/gender-equity-2022, accessed 15 July 2024
80 ONS, 'Gender pay gap in the UK: 2023' (1 November 2023), www.ons.gov.uk/employmentandlabourmarket/peopleinwork/earningsandworkinghours/bulletins/genderpaygapintheuk/2023, accessed 23 August 2024
81 Ibid
82 R Kochhar, 'The enduring grip of the gender pay gap', *Pew Research Center* (1 March 2023), www.pewresearch.org/social-trends/2023/03/01/the-enduring-grip-of-the-gender-pay-gap, accessed 15 July 2024; K Haan, 'Top gender pay gap statistics', *Forbes* (1 March 2024), www.forbes.com/advisor/business/gender-pay-gap-statistics, accessed 15 July 2024
83 European Commission, 'The gender pay gap situation in the EU' (2022), https://commission.europa.eu/strategy-and-policy/policies/justice-and-fundamental-rights/gender-equality/equal-pay/gender-pay-gap-situation-eu_en, accessed 15 July 2024; European Commission, 'Gender pay gap in the EU remains at 13% on Equal Pay Day' (14 November 2023), https://ec.europa.eu/commission/presscorner/detail/en/statement_23_5692, accessed 5 July 2024

84 World Bank, 'Beyond equal pay' (2020), https://blogs. worldbank.org/en/developmenttalk/beyond-equal-pay, accessed 15 July 2024
85 Equal Measures 2030, *Findings from the 2024 SDG Gender Index: A gender equal future in crisis?* (2024), https://equalmeasures2030.org/2024-sdg-gender-index, accessed 5 October 2024
86 In 2022–2023 there were 215,570 new-build homes completed, which is 70.8% of the Labour government's 300,000 homes per year target. Department for Levelling Up, Housing and Communities, 'Housing supply: Net additional dwellings, England: 2022 to 2023' (November 2023), www.gov.uk/government/statistics/housing-supply-net-additional-dwellings-england-2022-to-2023/housing-supply-net-additional-dwellings-england-2022-to-2023, accessed 24 August 2024
87 J Egan, *Rethinking Construction ('The Egan Report')* (1998), paragraph 4, https://constructingexcellence.org.uk/rethinking-construction-the-egan-report, accessed 9 February 2025
88 CITB, *CSN Industry Outlook – 2024–2028* (15 May 2024), www.citb.co.uk/about-citb/construction-industry-research-reports/construction-skills-network-csn, accessed 23 February 2025
89 FE News, '1 in 4 women open to skilled trades, Trade-Up research reveals' (26 June 2023), www.fenews.co.uk/skills/1-in-4-women-open-to-skilled-trades-trade-up-research-reveals, accessed 23 February 2025
90 *Professional Builder Podcast* (12 December 2023), https://player.captivate.fm/episode/41a436b7-b4b0-44f5-a35e-dcf483d792f2, accessed 21 December 2023
91 On the Tools, *Closing the Gap: Tackling the skills shortage* (2022), www.onthetools.tv/home/skills-shortage-white-paper, accessed 16 January 2024
92 On the Tools, *A Research Document Into Women in Construction: 2022*, www.fischer.co.uk/-/media/fixing-systems/rebrush/fiuk/white-papers-blog-post/wott-whitepaper.pdf, accessed 10 March 2024

93 T Menteth, '"We want access to decent toilets on site," say women across construction industry', *Ground Engineering* (16 February 2024), https://www.geplus.co.uk/news/we-want-access-to-decent-toilets-on-site-say-women-acros-sindustry-15-02-2024, accessed 10 March 2024

94 On The Tools, 'Why you should read the Women On The Tools white paper' (2022), www.onthetools.tv/sign-up-for-women-ott-white-paper, accessed 10 March 2024

95 PHPI, 'IWD: 39% of tradeswomen "aren't taken seriously"' (8 March 2022), https://phpionline.co.uk/news/iwd-39-of-tradeswomen-arent-taken-seriously, accessed 10 March 2024

96 Millennium Point, 'The gender gap in STEM education' (20 February 2023), www.millenniumpoint.org.uk/stem-education-2, accessed 10 March 2024

97 STEM Women, 'Women in STEM statistics: Progress and challenges' (30 August 2023), www.stemwomen.com/women-in-stem-statistics-progress-and-challenges, accessed 10 March 2024

98 D Bhatia et al, 'Women's body armor: A comprehensive review of design, performance, and ergonomics', *Journal of Engineered Fibers and Fabrics*, 19 (2024), https://journals.sagepub.com/doi/10.1177/15589250241232151?icid=int.sj-abstract.citing-articles.2, accessed 18 December 2024

99 Police Professional, 'Body armour for female officers to be evaluated as part of breast health trial' (14 June 2023), https://policeprofessional.com/news/body-armour-for-female-officers-to-be-evaluated-as-part-of-breast-health-trial, accessed 18 December 2024

100 L O'Dwyer, 'Why queues for women's toilets are longer than men's', *The Conversation* (23 August 2018), https://theconversation.com/why-queues-for-womens-toilets-are-longer-than-mens-99763, accessed 23 February 2025; R George, 'Why women face longer toilet queues – and how we can achieve "potty parity"', *The Guardian* (21 March 2018), www.theguardian.com/lifeandstyle/shortcuts/2018/mar/21/why-women-face-longer-toilet-queues-and-how-we-can-achieve-potty-parity, accessed 23 February 2025

101 O Theocharides-Feldman, 'Are girls being designed out of public spaces?', LSE (15 November 2022), www.lse.ac.uk/research/research-for-the-world/society/are-girls-being-designed-out-of-public-spaces, accessed 6 October 2024

102 HR News, '85% of UK women would change their commuting pattern to avoid the dark' (2023), https://hrnews.co.uk/85-of-uk-women-would-change-their-commuting, accessed 18 December 2024

103 V Heald, S Leadbetter and L Brooks, *Solving Transport's Diversity Disparity: Gender* (WSP, 2022), www.wsp.com/-/media/insights/uk/images/2022/towards-inclusive-travel-tackling-transport-gender-bias/solving-transports-diversity-disparity.pdf, accessed 6 October 2024

104 BCIS, 'Latest construction firm insolvency figures' (20 February 2025), https://bcis.co.uk/news/construction-insolvencies-latest-news, accessed 21 October 2024

105 R Nazzini and A Kalisz, *2022 Construction Adjudication in the United Kingdom: Tracing trends and guiding reform* (Centre of Construction Law and Dispute Resolution, King's College London, 2022), www.kcl.ac.uk/construction-law/assets/kcl-dpsl-construction-adjudication-report-a4-aw-june-2023-update.pdf, accessed 22 October 2024

106 R Nazzini and A Kalisz, *2023 Construction Adjudication in the United Kingdom: Tracing trends and guiding reform* (Centre of Construction Law and Dispute Resolution, King's College London, 2023), www.kcl.ac.uk/construction-law/assets/kcl-dpsl-construction-adjudication-report-2023-update-digital-aw.pdf, accessed 22 December 2023

107 World Health Organization, 'One in 100 deaths is by suicide' (17 June 2021), www.who.int/news/item/17-06-2021-one-in-100-deaths-is-by-suicide, accessed 8 September 2023

108 American Foundation for Suicide Prevention, *Suicide Data: United States* (2022), www.datocms-assets.com/12810/1649682186-14296_afsp_2022_national_fact_sheet_update_m1_v4.pdf, accessed 14 July 2024;

NOTES

      Samaritans, *Research Briefing: Gender and Suicide* (2020), https://media.samaritans.org/documents/ResearchBriefingGenderSuicide_2021_v7.pdf, accessed 1 July 2024

109 Samaritans, 'Suicides in England' (2021), https://media.samaritans.org/documents/Suicide_Stats_England_2021.pdf, accessed 8 September 2023

110 CIOB, *Understanding Mental Health in the Built Environment* (2020), www.ciob.org/media/48/download, accessed 14 July 2024

111 Lighthouse, 'ONS statistics show construction suicide rate increase in 2021' (5 December 2022), www.lighthouseclub.org/ons-statistics-show-construction-suicide-rate-increase-in-2021, accessed 7 March 2025

112 CPWR, 'Mental health in the construction industry: Resources to prevent suicide deaths in construction' (2024), www.cpwr.com/research/research-to-practice-r2p/r2p-library/other-resources-for-stakeholders/mental-health-addiction/suicide-prevention-resources, accessed 14 July 2024

113 Mates in Construction, 'Why MATES exists: The problem', https://mates.org.au/construction/the-problem, accessed 14 July 2024

114 InfoFinland.fi, 'Holidays and leave' (21 January 2025), www.infofinland.fi/en/work-and-enterprise/during-employment/holidays-and-leaves, accessed 7 March 2025

115 *The Guardian*, 'Finnish fathers taking nearly double length of paternity leave since 2022 reform' (7 November 2024), www.theguardian.com/world/2024/nov/07/finnish-fathers-paternity-leave-finland, accessed 7 November 2024

116 HR Grapevine, 'Benefits boost: Marks & Spencer announces biggest ever investment in pay and family leave policies' (29 February 2024), www.hrgrapevine.com/content/article/2024-02-29-marks-spencer-announces-biggest-ever-investment-in-pay-family-leave-policies, accessed 29 October 2024

117 Elliot Rae, 'The 74 UK employers offering equal parental leave' (2024), https://elliottrae.com/the-74-uk-employers-offering-equal-parental-leave, accessed 10 February 2025
118 M Travis, 'Why (and how) male allies should lean in to paternity leave', *Forbes* (30 January 2024), www.forbes.com/sites/michelletravis/2024/01/30/why-and-how-male-allies-should-lean-in-to-paternity-leave, accessed 10 October 2024
119 RJ Petts and C Knoester, 'Paternity leave-taking and father engagement', *Journal of Marriage and Family*, 80/5 (2018), https://pmc.ncbi.nlm.nih.gov/articles/PMC6124678, accessed 10 October 2024
120 Flexa, 'The Flexa100 is here' (2024), https://flexa.careers/flexa100, accessed 29 October 2024
121 4 Day Week, 'The 4 Day Week UK results' (2023), www.4dayweek.com/uk-pilot-results, accessed 15 April 2023
122 S Read, L Hooker and E Simpson, 'Firms stick to four-day week after trial ends', *BBC News* (21 February 2023), www-bbc-co-uk.cdn.ampproject.org/c/s/www.bbc.co.uk/news/business-64669987.amp, accessed 15 April 2023
123 A Benson, D Li and K Shue, '"Potential" and the gender promotion gap' (22 June 2022), https://danielle-li.github.io/assets/docs/PotentialAndTheGenderPromotionGap.pdf, accessed 5 October 2024
124 ME Heilman, 'Sex stereotypes and their effects in the workplace: What we know and what we don't know', *Journal of Social Behavior & Personality*, 10/6 (1995), 3–26
125 AH Eagly and SJ Karau, 'Role congruity theory of prejudice toward female leaders', *Psychological Review*, 109/3 (2002), 573
126 MA Sieghart, 'The Confidence Trick', in *The Authority Gap* (Black Swan, 2022)
127 G Whitty-Collins, *Why Men Win at Work: And how we can make inequality history* (Luath Press, 2021)

128 M McKinnon and C O'Connell, 'Perceptions of stereotypes applied to women who publicly communicate their STEM work', *Humanities and Social Sciences Communications*, 7 (2020), www.nature.com/articles/s41599-020-00654-0, accessed 5 October 2024

129 ManKind Initiative, 'Statistics on male victims of domestic abuse' (2023), https://mankind.org.uk/statistics/statistics-on-male-victims-of-domestic-abuse, accessed 23 February 2025; Consilia Legal, 'November highlights the unspoken truth of domestic violence against men' (18 November 2024), https://consilialegal.co.uk/november-highlights-the-unspoken-truth-of-domestic-violence-against-men, accessed 23 February 2025

130 K Magee, 'How female leaders are judged differently', *Management Today*, www.managementtoday.co.uk/female-leaders-judged-differently/women-in-business/article/1728242, accessed 7 March 2025; S O'Reilly, 'Why are women judged more harshly than men?' (28 March 2015), https://sallyoreilly.com/why-are-women-judged-more-harshly-then-men, accessed 7 March 2025; When Women Inspire, '9 things society judges women more harshly for than men' (2023), https://whenwomeninspire.com/2023/11/24/women-judged-gender-stereotypes/#google_vignette, accessed 7 March 2025; American Psychological Association, 'Women CEOs judged more harshly than men for corporate ethical failures' (24 October 2019), www.apa.org/news/press/releases/2019/10/corporate-ethical-failures, accessed 7 March 2025; C Weinberg, 'Patriarchy on trial: Double standards in the criminal justice system', *Revolving Doors* (1 March 2023), https://revolving-doors.org.uk/women-criminal-justice-double-standards, accessed 7 March 2025

131 C Rice, 'How McKinsey's story became Sheryl Sandberg's statistic - and why it didn't deserve to', *Huffington Post* (24 April 2014), www.huffingtonpost.co.uk/curt-rice/how-mckinseys-story-became-sheryl-sandbergs-statistic-and-why-it-didnt-deserve-to_b_5198744.html, accessed 15 October 2023

132 BIT, 'Women only apply when 100% qualified. Fact or fake news?' (8 March 2022), www.bi.team/blogs/women-only-apply-when-100-qualified-fact-or-fake-news, accessed 15 October 2023

133 MA Sieghart, *The Authority Gap* (Black Swan, 2022)

134 McKinsey & Company and Leanin.Org, *Women in the Workplace 2024*, www.mckinsey.com/featured-insights/diversity-and-inclusion/women-in-the-workplace, accessed 6 October 2024

135 UZH News, 'Women's Soccer Rated as Highly as Men's', *University of Zurich* (13 July 2023), www.news.uzh.ch/en/articles/media/2023/Women%e2%80%99s-Soccer-.html, accessed 8 September 2023

136 Gotherington Jaguars, www.facebook.com/gotheringtonjaguars, accessed 4 September 2023

137 Gotherington Jaguars (@gotheringtonjaguars), www.instagram.com/reel/CvxWM55tlar/?igsh=MWZxc28xd2Zvbjc3cw%3D%3D, accessed 10 February 2025

138 PR Clance and S Imes, 'The imposter phenomenon in high achieving women: Dynamics and therapeutic intervention', *Psychotherapy Theory, Research and Practice*, 15/3 (1978), www.paulineroseclance.com/pdf/ip_high_achieving_women.pdf, accessed 10 February 2025

139 MA Sieghart, 'The Confidence Trick', in *The Authority Gap* (Black Swan, 2022)

140 R Tulshyan and J-A Bure, 'Stop telling women they have imposter syndrome', *Harvard Business Review* (11 February 2021)

141 R Saujani, 'People ask me all the time: how do I overcome #ImposterSydrome?...' *LinkedIn* (2024), www.linkedin.com/posts/reshma-saujani_impostersyndrome-classof2023-bicycleface-activity-7067138536050708483-vy9_/?utm_source=share&utm_medium=member_ios, accessed 5 June 2023

142 S Hanlon, 'Bicycle face: A guide to Victorian cycling diseases' (4 January 2016), www.sheilahanlon.com/?p=1990, accessed 7 March 2025

NOTES

143 'The benefits of bicycling', *The Phrenological Journal and Science of Health,* 104 (1897) 274-275, https://books.google.co.uk/books?id=k9Y5AQAAMAAJ&pg=PA275&dq=%22bicycle+face%22&hl=en&sa=X&ei=fSG8U9eiCYSiyAS-kIEY&redir_esc=y#v=onepage&q&f=false, accessed 6 June 2023

144 Equal Measures 2030, *Findings from the 2024 SDG Gender Index: A gender equal future in crisis?* (2024), https://equalmeasures2030.org/wp-content/uploads/2024/08/EM2030_2024_SDG_Gender_Index.pdf, accessed 10 February 2025

145 Equality and Human Rights Commission, 'Pregnancy and maternity discrimination research findings' (25 May 2018), www.equalityhumanrights.com/guidance/business/pregnancy-and-maternity-discrimination-research-findings, accessed 5 October 2024

146 Fawcett Society, *Paths to Parenthood: Uplifting new mothers at work* (2023), www.fawcettsociety.org.uk/Handlers/Download.ashx?IDMF=d73d0c92-19af-479c-a206-0807ec008bf1, accessed 5 October 2024

147 If you feel you are suffering from discrimination or need advice, get in touch with them: https://pregnantthenscrewed.com/about-maternity-discrimination, accessed 11 February 2025

148 I am grateful to all those who then shared it with their networks; for example, I am aware that a recruitment headhunter I have known for years sent the questionnaire link to over 400 women in his database.

149 European Institute for Gender Equality, 'What is sexism', in *Sexism at Work: how can we stop it?* (2020), https://eige.europa.eu/publications-resources/toolkits-guides/sexism-at-work-handbook/part-1-understand/what-sexism?language_content_entity=en, accessed 13 September 2024

150 UN News, 'Report reveals nearly 90 per cent of all people have "a deeply ingrained bias" against women' (5 March 2020), https://news.un.org/en/story/2020/03/1058731, accessed 10 February 2025

151 Council of Europe, Preventing and Combating Sexism: Recommendation CM/Rec(2019)1 (2019), p21, https://rm.coe.int/prems-055519-gbr-2573-cmrec-2019-1-web-a5/168093e08c, accessed 13 September 2024

152 DJS Research, '73 per cent of engineers have faced gender discrimination' (6 February 2017), www.djsresearch.co.uk/EngineeringMarketResearchInsightsAndFindings/article/73-per-cent-of-engineers-have-faced-gender-discrimination-03475, accessed 10 February 2025; Construction News, 'Sexism "holding back" up to third of women in construction' (28 July 2017), www.constructionnews.co.uk/sections/news/sexism-holding-back-up-to-third-of-women-in-construction-28-07-2017, accessed 4 March 2023

153 H Waley-Cohen and D Fiandaca, *Sexualisation of Women in the Workplace* (2024), https://harrietwaleycohen.mykajabi.com/why-imposter-syndrome-is-a-dei-issue-opt-in-1, accessed 7 March 2025

154 www.legislation.gov.uk/ukpga/2003/42/section/3, accessed 18 December 2024

155 R Candlin, 'Tradeswomen paid less amid appalling sexism', *BBC News* (20 September 2024), www.bbc.co.uk/news/articles/c1k3k9y2dp3o, accessed 20 September 2024

156 I Weinfass, 'Why firms need an alcohol policy for industry events', *Construction News* (24 November 2023), www.constructionnews.co.uk/health-and-safety/why-firms-need-an-alcohol-policy-for-industry-events-24-11-2023, accessed 25 November 2023

157 *P v Crest Nicholson Operations Limited* (March 2023), Cambridge Employment Tribunal, https://assets.publishing.service.gov.uk/media/6475e44e5f7bb700127fa16b/P_v_Crest_Nicholson_Operations_Limited_3311744.2020___others_FMH_Reserved_Judgment.pdf, accessed 24 November 2023

158 Melissa Petro, 'I'm a female construction manager. I've had men comment on my looks and tell me I belong in the kitchen – but I still love my career', *Business Insider*

(8 February 2023), www.businessinsider.com/what-its-like-to-be-female-construction-manager-sexism-2023-2, accessed 7 March 2025

159 On the Tools, *A Research Document Into Women in Construction: 2022*, www.fischer.co.uk/-/media/fixing-systems/rebrush/fiuk/white-papers-blog-post/wott-whitepaper.pdf, accessed 10 March 2024

160 A Kaliszuk, 'I just got rejected for a job I'm beyond qualified for...', *LinkedIn*, www.linkedin.com/posts/ashleigh-kaliszuk_womeninconstruction-activity-7224454223147548672-j3z0?utm_source=share&utm_medium=member_ios, accessed 31 July 2024

161 'bully', *Cambridge Dictionary*, https://dictionary.cambridge.org/dictionary/english/bully, accessed 22 December 2023

162 Gov.uk, 'Workplace bullying and harassment', www.gov.uk/workplace-bullying-and-harassment, accessed 22 December 2023

163 Harassment is unlawful under the Equality Act 2010, section 26.

164 GMB Union, 'Just 3% of "blue collar" construction workers are women - GMB study' (24 June 2021), www.gmb.org.uk/news/just-3-blue-collar-construction-workers-are-women-gmb-study, accessed 6 October 2024

165 Herts Tool Co, 'The mental health in the construction industry survey 2021', https://hertstools.co.uk/mental-health-construction-industry-survey-2021, accessed 6 October 2024

166 L McLennan and W Morris, 'When does construction "banter" go too far?', *Construction Management* (6 January 2022), https://constructionmanagement.co.uk/when-does-banter-go-too-far, accessed 6 October 2024

167 G Whitty-Collins, *Why Men Win at Work: And how we can make inequality history* (Luath Press, 2021)

168 P Heim and SK Golant, *Hardball for Women: Winning at the game of business* (Plume, 2005)

169 R Billan, *The Tallest Poppy: How the workforce is cutting ambitious women down* (Women of Influence+,

2023), www.womenofinfluence.ca/wp-content/
uploads/2023/02/tp-whitepaper.pdf, accessed
25 June 2023

170 A Phagura (Inclusion in Transport and Construction),
www.linkedin.com/in/anita-phagura?utm_
source=share&utm_campaign=share_via&utm_
content=profile&utm_medium=ios_app, accessed 10
February 2025

171 Rated People, 'Standing up for tradeswomen' (8
March 2022), www.ratedpeople.com/blog/home-
improvement-trends-report-2022-empowering-
tradeswomen#:~:text=More%20than%20one%20in%20
three,see%20they're%20a%20woman, accessed 10
October 2024

172 C Picton and T Johnson, 'Gender pay gap data
reveals clients buck the trend on putting women into
top jobs', *New Civil Engineer* (5 April 2023), www.
newcivilengineer.com/latest/gender-pay-gap-data-
reveals-clients-buck-the-trend-on-putting-women-
into-top-jobs-05-04-2023, accessed 23 February
2025

173 Careers After Babies, *Careers After Babies Report* (2023),
www.careersafterbabies.org/careers-after-babies-report,
accessed 8 September 2023

174 Men for Inclusion, E2W, Women on the Wharf
and The Diversity Project, *The Road to an Inclusive
Workplace* (2022), www.menforinclusion.com/wp-
content/uploads/2024/10/MFI-Lived-Experience-
Research-2022.pdf, accessed 3 February 2025

175 C Criado-Perez, *Invisible Women: Exposing data bias in a
world designed for men* (Vintage, 2020)

176 Z Phillips, 'One size does not fit all: Lack of proper
PPE for women is dangerous', *Construction Dive* (9
March 2023), www.constructiondive.com/news/
dangers-of-lack-proper-ppe-safety-equipment-for-
women-construction/644379/?trk=feed_main-feed-
card%E2%80%A6, accessed 10 April 2023

177 A Keefe, *Canadian Women's Experiences with Personal
Protective Equipment in the Workplace* (Canadian

Standards Association, 2022), www.csagroup.org/article/research/canadian-womens-experiences-with-personal-protective-equipment-in-the-workplace, accessed 30 October 2023

178 C Lago, 'HS2 apprentice awarded for developing PPE for Muslim women', CIOB People (12 February 2024), https://ciobpeople.com/hs2-apprentice-awarded-for-developing-ppe-for-muslim-women, accessed 18 December 2024

179 SHP, 'Inclusive PPE – more than protection?' (10 August 2023), www-shponline-co-uk.cdn.ampproject.org/c/s/www.shponline.co.uk/women-in-health-and-safety/inclusive-ppe-more-than-protection/amp, accessed 10 August 2023

180 N Buddoo, 'CIOB announces #PPEthatfits campaign', *CIOB People* (1 July 2023), https://ciobpeople.com/new-ciob-campaign-on-ppe-in-construction, accessed 4 September 2023

181 The Construction (Design and Management) Regulations 2015, Schedule 2, www.legislation.gov.uk/uksi/2015/51/schedule/2/made, accessed 31 October 2023

182 Health and Safety Executive, 'Provision of welfare facilities during construction work', Construction Information Sheet No 59, p2, www.hse.gov.uk/pubns/cis59.pdf, accessed 11 February 2025. This now states that sanitary waste disposal should be provided in facilities used by female workers.

183 J Siebel Newsom, *Miss Representation* (Girls' Club Entertainment, 2011)

184 BJ King and J Howard, *All In: An autobiography* (Viking, 2021)

185 FTSE Women Leaders, *FTSE Women Leaders Review: Achieving gender balance* (2024), https://ftsewomenleaders.com/wp-content/uploads/2024/04/ftse-women-leaders-report-final-april-2024.pdf, accessed 5 October 2024

186 E Hinchliffe, 'The share of Fortune 500 companies run by women CEOs stays flat at 10.4% as pace of

change stalls', *Fortune* (4 June 2024), https://fortune.com/2024/06/04/fortune-500-companies-women-ceos-2024, accessed 5 October 2024

187   FTSE Women Leaders, *FTSE Women Leaders Review: Achieving gender balance* (2023), https://ftsewomenleaders.com/wp-content/uploads/2023/03/ftse-women-leaders-review-report-2022-v2.pdf, accessed 3 March 2023

188   L Haynes, 'Costain adds fifth female director to exec board', *Construction News* (21 October 2022), www.constructionnews.co.uk/news/peoplemoves-news/costain-adds-fifth-female-director-to-exec-board-21-10-2022, accessed 3 March 2023

189   Creditsafe, *Exploring Women in Business: Statistics and Trends for 2024* (2004), www.creditsafe.com/gb/en/blog/reports/women-in-business-2024.html, accessed 5 October 2024

190   Construction News, 'Unbalanced mix: the lack of diversity on the top 20 UK firm's exec boards' (1 July 2024), www.constructionnews.co.uk/sections/long-reads/unbalanced-mix-the-lack-of-diversity-on-the-top-20-uk-firms-exec-boards-01-07-2024, accessed 5 July 2024

191   K Murray, 'Are the trades still "jobs for the boys"?', Irish Examiner (17 August 2021), www.irishexaminer.com/lifestyle/healthandwellbeing/arid-40360370.html, accessed 10 April 2023

192   A Cunningham, 'Girls "inspired" by women in construction event', *BBC News* (14 October 2024), www.bbc.com/news/articles/c5y3636ppeko, accessed 15 October 2024

193   T Summers Hargis and BritMums, *How To Stand Up To Sexism: Words for when enough is enough* (2021)

194   K Coyne, 'Builder Barbie ignites social media debate', CIOB People (21 August 2023), https://ciobpeople.com/builder-barbie-ignites-social-media-debate, accessed 10 February 2025

195   S Cohen-Hatton, *The Gender Bias: The barriers that hold women back, and how to break them* (Blink Publishing, 2023), Chapter 4.

NOTES

196 'privilege', Cambridge Dictionary, https://dictionary.cambridge.org/dictionary/english/privilege, accessed 3 June 2023

197 Neurosculpting, 'Jo Britton', www.neurosculpting.com/find-a-facilitator/name/jo-britton, accessed 7 March 2025

198 MA Sieghart, *The Authority Gap* (Black Swan, 2022)

199 Kat Parsons, Head of Diversity, Equity and Inclusion at Centrica, is a global and multi-award winning D&I Speaker.

200 BBC Academy, *The Ally Track*, www.bbc.co.uk/creativediversity/creative-allies/allytrack, accessed 13 April 2025

201 Better Allies, '50 potential privileges in the workplace', https://betterallies.com/wp-content/uploads/2024/05/50-potential-privileges-in-the-workplace.pdf, accessed 13 July 2024

202 D Maitland, 'The day I learned I was part of the problem', *Moxy* (2024), www.themoxyvoice.com/leadership-stories/the-day-i-learned-i-was-part-of-the-problem, accessed 7 March 2025

203 L Bates, *Fix the System, Not the Women* (Simon & Schuster, 2023)

204 J Menasce Horowitz and R Igielnik, 'A century after women gained the right to vote, majority of Americans see work to do on gender equality', *Pew Research Center* (7 July 2020), www.pewresearch.org/social-trends/2020/07/07/a-century-after-women-gained-the-right-to-vote-majority-of-americans-see-work-to-do-on-gender-equality, accessed 7 September 2023

205 Ipsos, *International Women's Day 2023* (2023), www.ipsos.com/sites/default/files/ct/news/documents/2023-03/International%20Women%27s%20Day%202023%20-%20full%20report.pdf, accessed 7 September 2023

206 King's College London, 'Nearly half of Britons say women's equality has gone far enough' (4 March 2024), www.kcl.ac.uk/news/nearly-half-of-britons-say-womens-equality-has-gone-far-enough, accessed 12 July 2024

207 L Chambers, 'Allyship is nonsense…', *LinkedIn* (2024), www.linkedin.com/posts/leechambers-1_allyship-is-nonsense-its-womens-fault-activity-7215961557061529601-6NL8?utm_source=share&utm_medium=member_desktop, accessed 13 July 2024

208 K Catlin, *Better Allies* (Better Allies Press, 2021), https://betterallies.com, accessed 13 July 2024

209 PBC Today, 'Changing the narrative on suicide on World Suicide Prevention Day 2024' (10 September 2024), www.pbctoday.co.uk/news/health-safety-news/changing-narrative-suicide-world-suicide-prevention-day-2024, accessed 7 March 2025; ONS, 'Suicide by occupation, England and Wales, 2011 to 2020 registrations' (7 September 2021), www.ons.gov.uk/peoplepopulationandcommunity/birthsdeathsandmarriages/deaths/adhocs/13674suicidebyoccupationenglandandwales2011to2020registrations, accessed 7 March 2025; B Liversedge, 'Mental health in construction: Building the next storey', *British Safety Council* (8 February 2023), www.britsafe.org/safety-management/2023/mental-health-in-construction-building-the-next-storey, accessed 7 March 2025

210 Lighthouse, 'ONS Statistics Show Construction Suicide Rate Increase in 2021' (5 December 2022), www.lighthouseclub.org/ons-statistics-show-construction-suicide-rate-increase-in-2021, accessed 7 March 2025

211 G Laws, 'Largest-Ever UK Data Survey on Employee Diversity', *Supply Chain Sustainability School* (1 February 2023), www.supplychainschool.co.uk/diversity-survey-results-2022, accessed 1 June 2023

212 CITB, 'About the CITB levy', www.citb.co.uk/levy-grants-and-funding/citb-levy/about-the-citb-levy, accessed 22 September 2024

213 RICS, 'Built environment sector bodies unite to improve diversity and inclusion' (27 April 2022), www.rics.org/news-insights/built-environment-sector-bodies-unite-to-improve-diversity-equity-and-inclusion, accessed 22 September 2024

214 Vercida, 'Flexible, family-friendly policies at Aviva', www.vercida.com/uk/features/flexible-family-friendly-policies-at-aviva#:~:text=In%20the%20UK%2C%20we%20offer,first%20day%20a%20little%20easier, accessed 13 October 2024

215 S Forsdick, 'Spotify's CHRO on the return-to-office debate, layoffs and HR's changing role', *Raconteur* (7 October 2024), www.raconteur.net/talent-culture/spotify-chro-office-return-layoffs-hr-role, accessed 7 October 2024

216 B Liversedge, 'Where is SHE?', British Safety Council (3 July 2018), www.britsafe.org/safety-management/2019/where-is-she, accessed 27 March 2023

217 Steffan Battle, Executive Managing Director, showed me a video of the actors which also showed the leadership team watching the film; they were clearly shocked but the outcome was positive.

218 Kier, 'Diversity and inclusion', www.kier.co.uk/who-we-are/life-at-kier/diversity-and-inclusion, accessed 1 June 2023

219 T Thomas-Alexander, 'Kier sees rise in applicants since implementing family-friendly policies', *Construction News* (30 March 2022), www.constructionnews.co.uk/contractors/kier/kier-sees-rise-in-applicants-since-implementing-family-friendly-policies-30-03-2022, accessed 1 June 2023

220 Ibid

221 J Stein, 'Kier launches "returnship" for career-break workers', *Construction News* (18 January 2023), www.constructionnews.co.uk/skills/kier-launches-returnship-for-career-break-workers-18-01-2023, accessed 6 September 2023

222 Laing O'Rourke, 'Laing O'Rourke launches industry-leading global parental leave policy' (27 July 2022), www.laingorourke.com/company/news/2022/laing-o-rourke-launches-industry-leading-global-parental-leave-policy, accessed 7 March 2025; J Stein, 'Laing O'Rourke launches new equal parenting approach', *Construction*

News (28 July 2022), www.constructionnews.co.uk/contractors/laing-orourke/laing-orourke-launches-new-equal-parenting-approach-28-07-2022, accessed 3 March 2023

223 Laing O'Rourke, 'Gender equality action plan', www.laingorourke.com/media/apvjydlu/2024-gender_equality_action_plan.pdf, accessed 1 November 2024

224 Information provided directly by a TfL employee with whom I worked a few years ago.

225 Timewise, *Making Construction a Great Place to Work: Can flexible working help?* (2021), https://timewise.co.uk/wp-content/uploads/2021/06/TW-Making-construction-a-great-place-to-work-report.pdf, accessed 18 October 2024

226 Timewise, *Improving Flexible Working in Construction: A ten-point action plan* (2021), https://timewise.co.uk/wp-content/uploads/2021/06/TW-Construction-10-point-plan-for-flexible-working.pdf, accessed 11 February 2025

227 https://infrastructure-matters.co.uk/wp-content/uploads/2023/09/Women-in-Infrastructure.pdf, accessed 6 October 2024

228 World Economic Forum, 'Elizabeth Broderick has persuaded more than 260 executives…', *LinkedIn*, www.linkedin.com/posts/world-economic-forum_iwd24-activity-7173422796784549888-6GjQ, accessed 13 September 2024

229 Precise numbers: 240 said no, 60 said yes, and 2 said not applicable. It is unclear why two women said not applicable but this could have been because they were self-employed, meaning business DEI targets would not apply.

230 Any women wanting to look into the course go to https://thepowerwithintraining.com/construction-based-courses, accessed 7 March 2025

231 D Clarke, www.linkedin.com/in/dannymclarke, accessed 10 February 2025

NOTES

232 *The Guardian*, 'Andy Murray corrects journalist for overlooking female players – video' (13 July 2017), www.theguardian.com/sport/video/2017/jul/13/andy-murray-corrects-journalist-wimbledon-overlooking-female-video, accessed 1 September 2024

233 I Wright, 'Women's Football, Because of Men, Has Been Put Back', *British GQ* (15 July 2024), www.youtube.com/watch?v=46BTouxpnj0, accessed 10 February 2025

234 A Cripps, 'Why We Need More Male Allyship in Women's Football', *Versus* (4 July 2022), www.versus.uk.com/articles/why-we-need-more-male-allyship-in-womens-football, accessed 13 August 2023

235 Ugo Monye, 'The importance of male allies in women's sport', *The News Movement* (17 June 2023), www.youtube.com/watch?v=L5OnmahYlq0#:~:text=I'm%20a%20sports%20fan%2C%20and%20sport%20doesn't,Monye%20is%20a%20passionate%20male%20ally%20for, accessed 7 March 2025

236 The Sport Feed, 'Ugo Monye: On being a strong male ally for women's sport' (1 March 2022), www.thesportfeed.com/ugo-monye-on-being-a-strong-male-ally-for-womens-sport/#:~:text=Ugo%20Monye%20is%20former%20Harlequins,Sue%20Anstiss%20MBEUgo%20Monye, accessed 7 March 2025

237 ILM is the Institute of Leadership and Management, a UK provider of leadership, coaching and management qualifications and training, part of City & Guilds since November 2021. Humanise Solutions, 'Learning and development', www.humanisesolutions.com/service/learning-development/#certified, accessed 10 February 2025

238 Potentia and Token Man, *Men Leaning In Survey: Stories of success* (2022), https://static1.squarespace.com/static/598d8fb5e3df28d7f216e464/t/636a594a9055480b6c8f1697/1667914069392/EngagingMenStoriesofSuccess%28Nov22%29.pdf, accessed 13 July 2024

239 L Chambers, www.linkedin.com/in/leechambers-1/?originalSubdomain=uk, accessed 10 February 2025

240 P Murray, 'Not all men' (2023), https://youtu.be/AGdYa9frFG0?si=NWbDNHIWaoAGF5Nq, accessed 10 February 2025

241 S Naseem, 'This isn't on women…', *LinkedIn* (2024), www.linkedin.com/posts/sal-naseem_werisebyliftingeachother-mvawg-activity-7137712218061565952-3Kph/?utm_source=share&utm_medium=member_ios, accessed 10 February 2025

242 M Krentz et al, 'Five Ways Men Can Improve Gender Diversity at Work', BCG (10 October 2017), www.bcg.com/publications/2017/people-organization-behavior-culture-five-ways-men-improve-gender-diversity-work, accessed 18 December 2024

243 'dominate', Cambridge Dictionary, https://dictionary.cambridge.org/dictionary/english/dominate?q=dominated, accessed 10 February 2025

244 The UK offers just two weeks of statutory leave for new fathers paid at a measly £184.03/week or 90% of average weekly earnings, whichever is lower. This has the effect of precluding most men from being able to take time off as they can't afford it and those that do often struggle financially.

245 L Perry, 'Are crane operator breaks feasible?', *Crane Equipment Guide* (6 February 2023), www.craneequipmentguide.com/article/59819-are-crane-operator-breaks-feasible, accessed 4 June 2023

246 DM Munro, ME Govers and ML Oliver, 'Physical demands of overhead crane operation', *International Journal of Industrial Ergonomics*, 86 (2021), www.sciencedirect.com/science/article/abs/pii/S0169814121001189, accessed 4 June 2023

247 European Agency for Safety and Health at Work, *Prolonged Static Sitting at Work: Health effects and good practice advice* (2021), https://osha.europa.eu/en/publications/summary-prolonged-static-sitting-work-health-effects-and-good-practice-advice, accessed 4 June 2023

248 Project Implicit, *Implicit Association Test*, https://implicit.harvard.edu/implicit/takeatest.html, accessed 14 July 2024; Heineken, 'Worlds apart' (2017), www.youtube.com/watch?v=z3a8MdloAAM, accessed 10 February 2025

249 D Clark, 'Number of small and medium-sized enterprises in the United Kingdom in 2024, by sector', *Statista* (7 October 2024), www.statista.com/statistics/291210/sme-small-and-medium-enterprises-united-kingdom-uk-by-sector, accessed 17 July 2024

Further Reading

Bates, L, *Fix the System, Not the Women* (Simon & Schuster, 2023)

Beaulieu, S, *Breaking the Silence Habit: A practical guide to uncomfortable conversations in the #MeToo workplace* (Berrett-Koehler, 2020)

Chamorro-Premuzic, T, *Why Do So Many Incompetent Men Become Leaders? (And how to fix it)* (Harvard Business Review Press, 2019)

Cohen-Hatton, S, *The Gender Bias: The barriers that hold women back, and how to break them* (Blink Publishing, 2023)

Criado-Perez, C, *Invisible Women: Exposing data bias in a world designed for men* (Vintage, 2020)

Fanshawe, S, *The Power of Difference: Where the complexities of diversity and inclusion meet practical solutions* (Kogan Page, 2021)

Farque, P, *Inclusion: The ultimate secret for an organization's success* (2021)

Gail, L, *Extraordinary Women In History: 70 remarkable women who made a difference, inspired and broke barriers* (2021)

Garrod, C, *Conscious Inclusion: How to 'do' EDI, one decision at a time* (Practical Inspiration, 2023)

Malhotra, RT and Oluo, I, *Inclusion on Purpose: An intersectional approach to creating a culture of belonging at work* (The MIT Press, 2022)

McCann, J and McCann, K, *From Diversity to Inclusion: The power of leadership and team building* (Green Leaf Leadership, 2023)

McGuire, M, *The Female Edge: Accelerate your leadership ambition and craft a career on your own terms* (2021)

McGuire, M, *The Inclusion Edge: Confidently create a culture that celebrates diversity and belonging* (2022)

Moran, C, *How to Be a Woman* (Ebury Press, 2012)

Moran, C, *What about Men?* (Ebury Press, 2024)

Murray D, *The Madness of Crowds: Gender, race and identity* (Bloomsbury, 2020)

Neal, L, *Valued at Work: Shining a light on bias to engage, enable, and retain women in STEM* (Practical Inspiration, 2023)

Ramroop, M, *Building Inclusion: A practical guide to equity, diversity and inclusion in architecture and the built environment* (Routledge, 2024)

Sieghart, MA, *The Authority Gap* (Black Swan, 2022)

Summers Hargis, T and BritMums, *How to Stand Up to Sexism: Words for when enough is enough* (2021)

Syed, M, *Bounce: The myth of talent and the power of practice* (Fourth Estate, 2011)

Syed, M, *Rebel Ideas: The power of thinking differently* (John Murray, 2021)

Walsh, S, *Inclusive Leadership: Navigating organisational complexity* (2024)

Wambach, A, *Wolfpack: How to come together, unleash our power and change the game* (Piatkus, 2019)

Whittle, S and Bates, D, *Tough To Talk: Reducing male suicide and destroying the stigma one story at a time* (2024)

Whitty-Collins, G, *Why Men Win at Work: And how we can make inequality history* (Luath Press, 2021)

Acknowledgements

Too many men have had an impact on me to note them all here, and many are mentioned throughout the book, but I have to say a special thanks to two important men in my life: my father, John William Allen, the man who encouraged me to enter this industry in the first place; and second to my first manager, Gary Mumford, who coached me when I turned up as part of his team at eighteen years old and who continues to be a dear friend and mentor to this day. Without these two men cheering me on, I would have given up long ago and not stayed in the industry I love so much.

Thanks also to Daniel for helping to make the publication of this book a reality.

I want to thank those I have spoken to or whom have had an influence on me that led to me writing this book or helped in some way. There are many others who chose to remain anonymous, and I thank them too.

John Allen senior, John Allen junior, Felicity Allen, Simon Allen, Fraser Bishop, Jess Badley, Lesley Wright, Jude Bryant, Gary Mumford, Anna Doherty, Daniel Doherty, David Culliton, Maria Joyce, Phil Shortman, Dave Smith, Graham Shaw, Teresa Webster, James Duffy, Laurence Cobb, Anne Whitehouse, Yvonne Raleigh, Jayne Little, Christina Riley, Sam Maddock, Era Shah, Jessey Gomes, Chris Anderson, Mark Lewis, Richard Willmott-Smith KC, Karen Gough KC, Sapna Pieroux, Natasha Ozybko MBA, Charlie Woodley, James Taylor, Yolanda Walker, Katie Smith, Lisa Martello, Andy Pritchard, Charlotte Hamman, Chloe Fox, Rebecca Lambert, Jan Cruickshank, Kim Franklin KC, Alan Whaley, Anneliese Day KC, Iris Umiten, Yosof Ewing, Ian Weinfass, Michael Fisher, Chantelle Jalland, the Honourable Richard Evans, Tricia Estacio, Bonnie Moore, Michelle Minnikin, Helen Rowe, Aileen Out, Toby Mildon, Cerys Nelm, Antonia Nicol, Monica Christopher, Gillian Charlesworth, Mari Steyn, Nicky Thackray, Dr Jessica Taylor, Mark Freed, Susan O'Connor, Dr Roni Savage, Bron Williams, Jo Phillips, Helen Pamley, Catrin Rees, Rick Cooper, Marion Smith KC, Steve Whittle, Helen Rowe, Victoria (Lawrence) Russell, Diana Crouch OBE, Sophie Turner, SJK.

To the Rethink team – Joe Gregory, Geraldine Brennan, Anke Ueberg, Kathleen Steeden and the wider editing team – thank you for helping make

ACKNOWLEDGEMENTS

this happen! To my incredible Rethink mentor Lucy McCarraher, we finally got there; thank you for your unwavering support through my personal and professional challenges and many tears along the way that meant this took way longer than anticipated. Your faith and support helped keep me on track more than you know.

Thank you to Shane Miller for my author picture and Asis Patel for his amazing illustrations. A huge thank you to my beta readers: Amy Bonczyk, Steffan Battle, Lee Chambers, Sybil Taunton, and Jeremy Stockdale. Your feedback and advice is appreciated and helped this book be the best it could be.

The Author

Faye is a chartered quantity surveyor and Fellow of the RICS, a RICS Accredited Expert Witness, a Practising Member of the Academy of Experts, a Freeman of the City of London, member of the Worshipful Company of Arbitrators, Global Steering Committee member of the Equal Representation of Expert Witnesses (ERE) and Patron of WITBE GLOBAL Women in the Built Environment.

Faye has worked in construction for over thirty years and has significant knowledge of the construction process from the first twenty years of her career working for various contractors as a quantity surveyor and commercial manager running large and varied teams on multimillion-pound projects from inception to completion. She has worked in numerous sectors, including residential (housing, university accommodation and flats/apartments), commercial, large scale mixed-use developments, education, hotels, healthcare, power plants, shipbuilding, aviation, rail, sports stadiums and renewables, and still regularly undertakes independent advisory work on live projects. She now supports a variety of construction and engineering clients to avoid, mitigate and resolve disputes and is regularly involved in dispute resolution processes both domestically and internationally. Faye is experienced in providing expert evidence and witness evidence in high value/ high profile disputes and has given expert evidence and been cross examined by leading counsel in the Technology and Construction Court.

Alongside her work, Faye's passion is to improve the world for women and men alike. She campaigns for change to improve the representation of women in the industry and for people to work together to improve the culture so that everyone in construction can win.

🌐 https://buildingwomen.co.uk

in https://uk.linkedin.com/in/fayeallen